Hey, Andrew! Teach Me Some Greek!

A BIBLICAL GREEK WORKTEXT

LEVEL 4

BY KAREN MOHS

Dear Parent/Teacher:

Welcome to Greek Workbook Level Four!

In this Level Four workbook, students review the Greek alphabet, vocabulary, and grammar presented in Levels One through Three. They learn the forms of the Greek article, rules of accent, word order, and punctuation. In addition, feminine nouns are introduced, as well as additional vocabulary. The sentences are contrived and simplified to afford practice with the vocabulary and forms the student has learned.

Remove the flashcard pages at the end of the workbook, cut out the words, and copy, paste, or tape them onto 3 by 5 inch cards.

Practice reading orally in a Greek Interlinear New Testament, progressing through the Gospel of John. The student will continue to recognize words, with their various endings, and will become increasingly familiar with the flow of koiné Greek sentences and thought. Please read "Bible Copy Work" in the appendix.

Glossaries, paradigms, rules of accent, and an index are included for those who would find such resources useful.

An answer key is available, as well as quizzes/exams and flashcards on a ring. The audio pronunciation CD or cassette tape includes Greek letters, vocabulary, noun and verb paradigms, "The Greek Alphabet Song," and a reading of *The Reader*. For your convenience in completing Bible copy work, a Bible Copybook containing the entire Greek and interlinear English text of the Gospel of John is also available.

Keep having fun!

References:
   New Testament Greek For Beginners by J. Gresham Machen
   Essentials of New Testament Greek by Ray Summers
   A Short Syntax of New Testament Greek by H.P.V. Nunn
   Moods and Tenses of New Testament Greek by Earnest De Witt Burton
   A Manual Grammar of the Greek New Testament by Dana and Mantey
   Exhaustive Concordance of the Bible by James Strong

Copyright © 1995 by Karen Mohs
All rights reserved. No part of this publication may be reproduced without prior permission of the author.

ISBN-13: 978-1-931842-16-7
ISBN-10: 1-931842-16-7

Greek 'n' Stuff
P.O. Box 882
Moline, IL 61266-0882
www.greeknstuff.com

Revised 4/05

This Level Four Greek Workbook
belongs to:

Lauren Samantha Davis

(student's name)

TABLE OF CONTENTS

Lesson 1 1-6
    Alphabet review

Lesson 2 7-12
    Vocabulary review - Part 1

Lesson 3 13-16
    Vocabulary review - Part 2

Lesson 4 17-24
    Grammar review - Part 1

Lesson 5 25-32
    Grammar review - Part 2

Lesson 6 33-38
    New vocabulary - Part 1, vocabulary practice

Lesson 7 39-44
    New vocabulary - Part 2, vocabulary practice

Lesson 8 45-48
    New vocabulary - Part 3, vocabulary practice

Lesson 9 49-54
    The masculine article - singular and plural

Lesson 10 55-58
    The neuter article - singular and plural

Lesson 11 59-64
    New vocabulary - Part 4, vocabulary practice

Lesson 12 65-70
    New vocabulary - Part 5, vocabulary practice

Lesson 13 71-76
    New vocabulary - Part 6, vocabulary practice

Lesson 14 77-78
    Vowels, diphthongs, iota subscripts

Lesson 15 79-80
    Breathings, accents

Lesson 16 81-84
    Syllables

Lesson 17 85-86
    The acute accent

Greek Workbook - Level 4
Copyright © 1995 by Karen Mohs

Lesson 18 87-90
   The circumflex accent

Lesson 19 91-92
   The grave accent

Lesson 20 93-94
   Rule of verb accent

Lesson 21 95-98
   Rule of noun accent

Lesson 22 99-100
   Word order, punctuation

Lesson 23 101-106
   New vocabulary - Part 7, vocabulary practice

Lesson 24 107-114
   New vocabulary - Part 8, vocabulary practice

Lesson 25 115-120
   Feminine nouns, feminine first declension (long α) - singular

Lesson 26 121-124
   New vocabulary - Part 9, vocabulary practice

Lesson 27 125-128
   Feminine first declension (short α) - singular

Lesson 28 129-134
   New vocabulary - Part 10, vocabulary practice

Lesson 29 135-140
   New vocabulary - Part 11, vocabulary practice

Lesson 30 141-144
   New vocabulary - Part 12, vocabulary practice

Lesson 31 145-148
   Feminine first declension (η) - singular

Lesson 32 149-152
   Feminine first declension - plural

Lesson 33 153-158
   New vocabulary - Part 13, vocabulary practice

Lesson 34 159-160
   Feminine second declension - singular and plural

Lesson 35 161-165
   Final review - Part 1

Lesson 36 166-170
   Final review - Part 2

Appendix

Greek - English Glossary 171-172

English - Greek Glossary 173

Greek Alphabet 175

Vowels and Diphthongs 175

Punctuation 176

Breathing Marks 176

Word Order 176

Syllables 177

Accents 177

Rules of Accent 178

Moods of the Greek Verb 179

Voices of the Greek Verb 179

Present Tense 179

The Article 180

Gender of the Greek Noun 180

Cases of the Greek Noun 180

First Declension 181-182

Second Declension 183

Bible Copy Work 184

Index 185-186

Flashcard Tips 187

Greek Workbook - Level 4
Copyright © 1995 by Karen Mohs

Lesson 1

Feb. 24, 2021

GREEK ALPHABET REVIEW

ALPHA
α

Write the letter *alpha* (**al**-fa) across each line.

α α α α α α α α α α

α α α α α α α α α α

BETA
β

Write the letter *beta* (**bay**-ta) across each line.

β β β β β β β β β β β

β β β β β β β β β β β

GAMMA
γ

Write the letter *gamma* (**gam**-ma) across each line.

γ γ γ γ γ γ γ γ γ γ

γ γ γ γ γ γ γ γ γ γ

DELTA
δ

Write the letter *delta* (**del**-ta) across each line.

δ δ δ δ δ δ δ δ δ

δ δ δ δ δ δ δ δ δ

EPSILON
ε

Write the letter *epsilon* (**ep**-si-lon) across each line.

ε ε ε ε ε ε ε ε ε ε

ε ε ε ε ε ε ε ε ε ε

ZETA
ζ

Write the letter *zeta* (**zay**-ta) across each line.

ζ ζ ζ ζ ζ ζ ζ ζ ζ ζ

ζ ζ ζ ζ ζ ζ ζ ζ ζ ζ

Greek Workbook - Level 4
Copyright © 1995 by Karen Mohs

GREEK ALPHABET REVIEW

Write the letter *eta* (**ay**-ta) across each line.

ETA
η

Write the letter *theta* (**thay**-ta) across each line.

THETA
θ

Write the letter *iota* (ee-**o**-ta) across each line.

IOTA
ι

Write the letter *kappa* (**kap**-pa) across each line.

KAPPA
κ

Write the letter *lambda* (**lamb**-da) across each line.

LAMBDA
λ

Write the letter *mu* (**moo**) across each line.

MU
μ

2

Greek Workbook - Level 4
Copyright © 1995 by Karen Mohs

GREEK ALPHABET REVIEW

NU
ν

Write the letter *nu* (**noo**) across each line.

Write the letter *xi* (**ksee**) across each line.

XI
ξ

OMICRON
ο

Write the letter *omicron* (**ahm**-i-cron) across each line.

PI
π

Write the letter *pi* (**pie**) across each line.

RHO
ρ

Write the letter *rho* (**row**) across each line.

SIGMA
σ ς
(beginning or middle of word) (end of word)

Write the letter *sigma* (**sig**-ma) across each line.

Greek Workbook - Level 4
Copyright © 1995 by Karen Mohs

3

GREEK ALPHABET REVIEW

Write the letter *tau* (**tou**) across each line.

Write the letter *upsilon* (**up**-si-lon) across each line.

Write the letter *phi* (**fee**) across each line.

Write the letter *chi* (**kee**) across each line.

Write the letter *psi* (**psee**) across each line.

Write the letter *omega* (o-**may**-ga) across each line.

| TAU |
| UPSILON |
| PHI |
| CHI |
| PSI |
| OMEGA |

GREEK ALPHABET REVIEW

Match the Greek letters to their names and to their sounds.

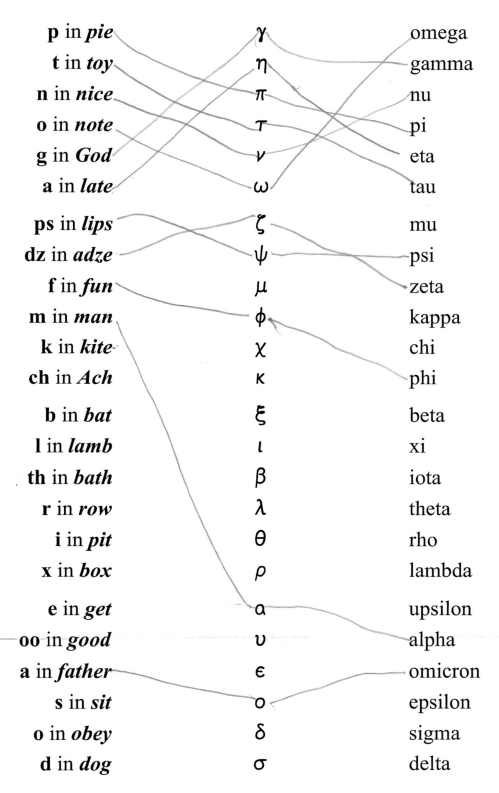

GREEK ALPHABET REVIEW

Write all twenty-four letters of the Greek alphabet in order.

Write the names of these Greek letters.

ξ _____   ρ _____

α _____   χ _____

φ _____   τ _____

κ _____   δ _____

σ _____   μ _____

λ _____   ψ _____

β _____   ζ _____

ι _____   ω _____

θ _____   ν _____

π _____   ο _____

ε _____   η _____

γ _____   υ _____

Lesson 2

VOCABULARY REVIEW

ὁ ἄνθρωπος

means

the man

It sounds like ho **an**-thro-pos.

Remember: The o and the ω both have a long o sound, but the ω is held longer.

Write **the man** in Greek.

Write **the brother** in Greek.

ὁ ἀδελφός

means

the brother

It sounds like
ho a-del-**fos**.

ὁ ἀπόστολος

means

the apostle

It sounds like
ho a-**po**-sto-los.

Write **the apostle** in Greek.

Write **I see** in Greek.

βλέπω

means

I see

It sounds like
ble-po.

☐ Flashcards - (Add the new cards. Check the box when you practice your flashcards.)
(See the back of this workbook for the flashcards.)

Greek Workbook - Level 4
Copyright © 1995 by Karen Mohs

7

VOCABULARY REVIEW

ἄνθρωπος means **a man**.

ὁ ἄνθρωπος means *the* **man**.

Write the word meaning **a man**.

Write the words meaning **the man**.

ἀδελφός means **a brother**.

ὁ ἀδελφός means *the* **brother**.

Write the word meaning **a brother**.

Write the words meaning **the brother**.

ἀπόστολος means **an apostle**.

ὁ ἀπόστολος means *the* **apostle**.

Write the word meaning **an apostle**.

Write the words meaning **the apostle**.

☐ Flashcards

8

VOCABULARY REVIEW

γινώσκω

means

I know

It sounds like
ghi-**no**-sko.

Write **I know** in Greek.

Write **and** in Greek.

καί

means

and

It sounds like
kahee.

ὁ δοῦλος

means

the slave, the servant

It sounds like
ho **doo**-los.

Write **the slave** in Greek.

Write **the word** in Greek.

ὁ λόγος

means

the word

It sounds like
ho **lo**-gos.

☐ Flashcards - (Add the new cards.)

Greek Workbook - Level 4
Copyright © 1995 by Karen Mohs

9

VOCABULARY REVIEW

Match the words to their meanings.

ἀδελφός   the brother

ὁ ἀδελφός   a brother

ἀπόστολος   an apostle

ὁ ἀπόστολος   the apostle

δοῦλος   the servant

ὁ δοῦλος   a servant

λόγος   the word

ὁ λόγος   a word

ἄνθρωπος   a man

ὁ ἄνθρωπος   the man

βλέπω —————————————and—

καί   I know

γινώσκω   I see

☐ Flashcards

VOCABULARY REVIEW

γράφω

means

I write

It sounds like
gra-fo.

Write **I write** in Greek.

Write **the son** in Greek.

ὁ υἱός

means

the son

It sounds like
ho hwee-**os**.

διδάσκω

means

I teach

It sounds like
di-**da**-sko.

Write **I teach** in Greek.

Write **the house** in Greek.

ὁ οἶκος

means

the house

It sounds like
ho **oy**-kos.

☐   Flashcards - (Add the new cards.)

Greek Workbook - Level 4
Copyright © 1995 by Karen Mohs

11

VOCABULARY REVIEW

Write the Greek words.

a word _____

I write _____

the son _____

the man _____

I teach _____

the house _____

a brother _____

I know _____

a servant _____

the word _____

a house _____

a son _____

the apostle _____

and _____

I see _____

the servant _____

☐ Flashcards

Lesson 3

VOCABULARY REVIEW

λέγω

means

I say

It sounds like
le-go.

Write **I say** in Greek.

Write **the law** in Greek.

ὁ νόμος

means

the law

It sounds like
ho **no**-mos.

ἔχω

means

I have

It sounds like
e-kho.

Write **I have** in Greek.

Write **the angel** in Greek.

ὁ ἄγγελος

means

the angel

It sounds like
ho **an**-ge-los.*

*When a gamma is followed by another gamma (or a kappa or a chi), the gamma is pronounced **ng**.

☐ Flashcards - (Add the new cards.)

Greek Workbook - Level 4
Copyright © 1995 by Karen Mohs

13

VOCABULARY REVIEW

Match the words to their meanings.

ὁ υἱός   a word

ὁ ἀπόστολος   an angel

ὁ ἄγγελος   the son

λόγος   the apostle

ἄγγελος   the angel

ἄνθρωπος   an apostle

ἀπόστολος   a man

υἱός   the word

ὁ λόγος   a son

ὁ δοῦλος   the law

ὁ νόμος   the servant

οἶκος   a brother

ἀδελφός   a house

ὁ ἄνθρωπος   a servant

δοῦλος   a law

νόμος   the man

ὁ ἀδελφός   the house

ὁ οἶκος   the brother

☐ Flashcards

14

Greek Workbook - Level 4
Copyright © 1995 by Karen Mohs

VOCABULARY REVIEW

λαμβάνω

means

I take

It sounds like
lam-**ba**-no.

Write **I take** in Greek.

Write **the gift** in Greek.

τὸ δῶρον

means

the gift

It sounds like
to **do**-ron.

ἀκούω

means

I hear

It sounds like
a-**koo**-o.

Write **I hear** in Greek.

Write **the temple** in Greek.

τὸ ἱερόν

means

the temple

It sounds like
to hee-e-**ron**.

☐ Flashcards - (Add the new cards.)

Greek Workbook - Level 4
Copyright © 1995 by Karen Mohs

15

VOCABULARY REVIEW

Circle the correct meanings.

ὁ ἀδελφός	a brother the man the brother	λόγος	a log a word a record
τὸ ἱερόν	the son the temple the bird	λέγω	I say I dance I leap
ἀπόστολος	an apostle an angel a brother	ὁ νόμος	the name the law the statue
βλέπω	I throw I believe I see	ἀκούω	I say I sneeze I hear
ὁ οἶκος	the house an onion the angel	τὸ δῶρον	the gift the room the temple
υἱός	a house a son a bus	διδάσκω	I act I sing I teach
λαμβάνω	I throw I carry I take	γινώσκω	I know I grow I have
ὁ ἄγγελος	the angel an angle the brother	ἔχω	I say I have I am
γράφω	I draw I write I graph	δοῦλος	a servant a sadness a man

☐ Flashcards

Lesson 4

DO YOU REMEMBER?

βλέπω means **I see.**   βλέπομεν means **We see.**

βλέπεις means **You** (singular) **see.**   βλέπετε means **You** (plural) **see.**

βλέπει means **He (she, it) sees.**   βλέπουσι means **They see.**

This conjugation is called the *present active indicative*.

Match the words to their meanings.

γινώσκει   I know

γινώσκεις   he knows

γινώσκω   you know

λαμβάνετε   you take

λαμβάνουσι   we take

λαμβάνομεν   they take

λέγει   you say

λέγω   I say

λέγετε   he says

ἔχουσι   they have

ἔχεις   you have

ἔχω   I have

ἀκούεις   they hear

ἀκούουσι   we hear

ἀκούομεν   you hear

☐ Flashcards - (Add the new cards.)

Greek Workbook - Level 4
Copyright © 1995 by Karen Mohs

17

LET'S PRACTICE

Write the meanings of the following Greek words.

λέγω _____

λέγεις _____

λέγει _____

ἀκούω _____

ἀκούεις _____

ἀκούει _____

λαμβάνω _____

λαμβάνεις _____

λαμβάνει _____

γινώσκω _____

γινώσκεις _____

γινώσκει _____

βλέπω _____

βλέπεις _____

βλέπει _____

ἔχω _____

ἔχεις _____

ἔχει _____

γράφομεν _____

διδάσκω _____

γράφω _____

λέγομεν _____

λέγετε _____

λέγουσι _____

ἀκούομεν _____

ἀκούετε _____

ἀκούουσι _____

λαμβάνομεν _____

λαμβάνετε _____

λαμβάνουσι _____

γινώσκομεν _____

γινώσκετε _____

γινώσκουσι _____

βλέπομεν _____

βλέπετε _____

βλέπουσι _____

ἔχομεν _____

ἔχετε _____

ἔχουσι _____

διδάσκει _____

γράφει _____

διδάσκεις _____

☐ Flashcards

18

Greek Workbook - Level 4
Copyright © 1995 by Karen Mohs

LET'S PRACTICE

Circle the correct words.

I teach	you say	we hear
διδάσκεις διδάσκει διδάσκω	λέγω λέγετε λέγομεν	ἀκούω ἀκούεις ἀκούομεν
you take	**we see**	**you see**
λαμβάνω λαμβάνετε λαμβάνει	βλέπομεν βλέπεις βλέπουσι	ἔχετε βλέπετε λαμβάνετε
he writes	**I know**	**you have**
γράφει γράφομεν γράφω	γινώσκετε γινώσκομεν γινώσκω	ἔχεις ἔχει ἔχω
he has	**we hear**	**they take**
λαμβάνει ἔχει διδάσκει	λέγομεν γράφομεν ἀκούομεν	λαμβάνεις λαμβάνουσι λαμβάνομεν
they know	**he hears**	**I see**
γινώσκουσι γινώσκει γινώσκεις	ἀκούει ἀκούουσι ἀκούετε	βλέπει βλέπετε βλέπω
you say	**we have**	**you teach**
λέγουσι λέγει λέγεις	ἔχετε ἔχομεν ἔχουσι	διδάσκεις ἀκούεις λέγεις

☐ Flashcards

Greek Workbook - Level 4
Copyright © 1995 by Karen Mohs

19

DO YOU REMEMBER?

βλέπει means **He sees.**

If we want to say **He sees *a man***, we write
βλέπει ἄνθρωπον.

If we want to say **He sees *men***, we write
βλέπει ἀνθρώπους.*

ἄνθρωπον and ἀνθρώπους are in the Greek *accusative* case.
Words in this case are called ***direct objects*** in English grammar.

Write the correct Greek words in these sentences.

1. _____

    It means **We see an angel.**

2. _____

    It means **They know servants.**

3. _____

    It means **He teaches sons.**

4. _____

    It means **You hear words.**

5. _____

    It means **I have a house and a brother.**

γινώσκουσι
καὶ
λόγους
ἄγγελον
ἔχω
δούλους*
διδάσκει
ἀδελφόν
βλέπομεν
υἱούς
οἶκον
ἀκούεις

*Rules for Accent will be taught later in this workbook. For now, learn the placement of the accent by observation of each individual word.

☐ Flashcards - (Add the new cards.)

DO YOU REMEMBER?

βλέπει ἀδελφόν means **He sees a brother.**

If we want to say **He sees a brother *of a man***, we write
βλέπει ἀδελφὸν* ἀνθρώπου.

If we want to say **He sees a brother *of men***, we write
βλέπει ἀδελφὸν ἀνθρώπων.

ἀνθρώπου and ἀνθρώπων are in the Greek *genitive* case.
The genitive case shows *possession*.

Circle the correct meanings of these Greek sentences.

γινώσκω δοῦλον ἀδελφοῦ.*	He knows servants of a brother. I know a servant of a brother. You know a servant of a brother.
λέγομεν λόγον ἀποστόλου.	We say a word of an apostle. They say words of apostles. I say a word of an apostle.
διδάσκεις υἱὸν δούλου.	He teaches a son of a slave. You teach sons of a slave. You teach a son of a slave.
ἀκούει νόμους ἀνθρώπων.	He hears a law of men. He hears laws of men. He hears laws of a man.

*Rules for Accent will be taught later in this workbook. For now, learn the placement of the accent by observation of each individual word.

☐ Flashcards - (Add the new cards.)

Greek Workbook - Level 4
Copyright © 1995 by Karen Mohs

21

DO YOU REMEMBER?

βλέπει ἀδελφόν means **He sees a brother.**

If we want to say ***An apostle* sees a brother**, we write

ἀπόστολος βλέπει ἀδελφόν.

ἀπόστολος is in the Greek ***nominative*** case. It is singular.
Words in this case are called ***subjects*** in English grammar.

Write the meanings of the Greek sentences on the lines beneath the sentences.

ἀκούει ἀγγέλους.	γινώσκει ἀπόστολον.
_____	_____
δοῦλος ἀκούει ἀγγέλους.	ἄνθρωπος γινώσκει ἀπόστολον.
_____	_____
γράφει νόμον.	λαμβάνει οἴκους.
_____	_____
ἄγγελος γράφει νόμον.	ἀδελφὸς λαμβάνει οἴκους.
_____	_____
βλέπει ἀποστόλους.	διδάσκει ἀδελφούς.
_____	_____
υἱὸς βλέπει ἀποστόλους.	νόμος διδάσκει ἀδελφούς.
_____	_____
λέγει λόγους.	ἔχει ἀνθρώπους.
_____	_____
ἀπόστολος λέγει λόγους.	οἶκος ἔχει ἀνθρώπους.
_____	_____

☐ Flashcards

22

Greek Workbook - Level 4
Copyright © 1995 by Karen Mohs

DO YOU REMEMBER?

βλέπουσι δοῦλον means **They see a slave.**

If we want to say ***Brothers* see a slave**, we write
ἀδελφοὶ βλέπουσι δοῦλον.

ἀδελφοί is in the Greek ***nominative*** case. It is plural.
Remember--words in this case are called ***subjects*** in English grammar.

Fill in the blanks with the correct Greek words. Write what the sentences mean.

1. ἄνθρωποι ἔχουσιν* _____.
   (brothers)

   It means _____

2. _____ ἀκούουσι καὶ βλέπουσιν.*
   (angels)

   It means _____

3. δοῦλοι λέγουσι _____ ἀποστόλων.
   (laws)

   It means _____

4. ἀδελφὸς γράφει λόγους _____.
   (of an apostle)

   It means _____

*The "moveable ν" is added to a word ending in ουσι if the following word begins with a vowel or if the word comes at the end of the clause or the end of the sentence. In the Greek New Testament, the moveable ν is sometimes used in other constructions. For now, simply follow the above rule.

☐ Flashcards - (Add the new cards.)

Greek Workbook - Level 4
Copyright © 1995 by Karen Mohs

23

DO YOU REMEMBER?

γράφω λόγους means **I write words.**

If we want to say **I write words** *to a man*

or **I write words** *for a man*, we write

γράφω λόγους ἀνθρώπῳ.*

If we want to say **I write words** *to men*

or **I write words** *for men*, we write

γράφω λόγους ἀνθρώποις.

ἀνθρώπῳ and ἀνθρώποις are in the Greek *dative* case.
Words in this case are called *indirect objects* in English grammar.

Put the endings in the boxes on the Greek words in the sentences.

οις ομεν ους οῖς	1. We have laws for apostles and for sons. ἔχ＿＿＿ νόμ＿＿＿ ἀποστόλ＿＿＿ καὶ υἱ＿＿＿ .	
οις ους οι ουσι	2. Men say words to servants. ἄνθρωπ＿＿＿ λέγ＿＿＿ λόγ＿＿＿ δούλ＿＿＿ .	
οι ον ω οῖς	3. I teach a law to brothers. διδάσκ＿＿＿ νόμ＿＿＿ ἀδελφ＿＿＿ .	
ους ομεν ον ομεν	4. We know an apostle and hear angels. γινώσκ＿＿＿ ἀπόστολ＿＿＿ καὶ ἀκού＿＿＿ ἀγγέλ＿＿＿ .	
ος ῷ ον ει	5. A servant has a house for a son. δούλ＿＿＿ ἔχ＿＿＿ οἶκ＿＿＿ υἱ＿＿＿ .	
ου ει ὸν ος	6. An angel sees a brother of a man. ἄγγελ＿＿＿ βλέπ＿＿＿ ἀδελφ＿＿＿ ἀνθρώπ＿＿＿ .	

*The iota subscript (ͺ) is written under certain long vowels instead of an iota after them.

☐ Flashcards - (Add the new cards.)

24

Lesson 5

DO YOU REMEMBER?

If we want to *tell* an angel that we see a house, we write

ἄγγελε, βλέπομεν οἶκον.

It means *Angel,* **we see a house.**

If we want to tell *more than one* angel, we write

ἄγγελοι, βλέπομεν οἶκον.

It means *Angels,* **we see a house.**

ἄγγελε and ἄγγελοι are in the Greek *vocative* case.
Words in this case are called *words of direct address* in English grammar.

Match the Greek sentences to their meanings.

_____ 1. υἱέ, γράφομεν λόγον.   a. Sons, we write a word.

_____ 2. υἱοί, γράφομεν λόγον.   b. Son, we write a word.

_____ 3. ἀπόστολος διδάσκει.   c. An apostle teaches.

_____ 4. διδάσκει ἀποστόλους.   d. He teaches apostles.

_____ 5. λαμβάνετε οἴκους.   e. You (singular) take houses.

_____ 6. λαμβάνεις οἴκους.   f. You (plural) take houses.

_____ 7. λέγει λόγους υἱῶν.   g. He says words to sons.

_____ 8. λέγει λόγους υἱοῖς.   h. He says words of sons.

_____ 9. γινώσκει δοῦλον.   i. A servant knows.

_____ 10. δοῦλος γινώσκει.   j. He knows a servant.

_____ 11. ἀδελφοί, ἔχω νόμον.   k. Brothers, I have a law.

_____ 12. ἀδελφέ, ἔχομεν νόμον.   l. Brother, we have a law.

_____ 13. λαμβάνει υἱὸν καὶ δούλους.   m. He takes a son of slaves.

_____ 14. λαμβάνει υἱὸν δούλων.   n. He takes a son and slaves.

☐ Flashcards - (Add the new cards.)

Greek Workbook - Level 4
Copyright © 1995 by Karen Mohs

25

LET'S PRACTICE

Circle the correct words. Write what the sentences mean.

1. λέγομεν λόγους νόμου υἱῷ καὶ (δοῦλοι, δούλῳ).

   It means _____

2. ἀπόστολοι (ἀκούουσιν, ἀκούω) ἀγγέλους καὶ βλέπουσιν υἱούς.

   It means _____

3. ἀδελφοὶ καὶ ἄνθρωποι (ἔχουσι, ἔχουσιν) νόμους.

   It means _____

4. διδάσκω υἱὸν δούλου, καὶ ἔχει (οἶκος, οἶκον).

   It means _____

5. ἀκούεις (ἀπόστολον, ἀπόστολος) καὶ βλέπεις δούλους ἀνθρώπων.

   It means _____

6. ἀδελφὸς (λέγουσι, λέγει) λόγους υἱοῖς ἀνθρώπου.

   It means _____

7. δοῦλος καὶ υἱοὶ (λαμβάνω, λαμβάνουσιν) οἴκους.

   It means _____

8. γράφομεν (νόμον, νόμῳ) δούλοις καὶ ἀδελφοῖς.

   It means _____

9. (ἄγγελος, ἄγγελοι) γινώσκει οἴκους ἀποστόλων καὶ δούλων.

   It means _____

10. (ἀδελφοί, ἀδελφέ), ἔχετε λόγον ἀδελφῷ καὶ ἀνθρώποις.

    It means _____

☐ Flashcards

LET'S PRACTICE

Draw lines to connect the parts of the sentences.

1. ἀπόστολος γράφει νόμους   καὶ δούλῳ.

2. λέγομεν λόγους καὶ ἀκούομεν   λαμβάνεις υἱούς.

3. ἀδελφοὶ καὶ υἱοὶ ἔχουσιν   ἀνθρώπῳ.

4. λέγω λόγον ἀδελφῷ   ἀγγέλους.

5. ἄνθρωπε,   οἴκους.

Now write the sentences you have made. First write them in Greek. Then write what they mean.

1. _____

   It means _____

2. _____

   It means _____

3. _____

   It means _____

4. _____

   It means _____

5. _____

   It means _____

☐ Flashcards

Greek Workbook - Level 4
Copyright © 1995 by Karen Mohs

LET'S PRACTICE

Choose the correct words for the sentences. Put them in the blanks. Write what the sentences mean.

ἔχετε - ἔχουσιν

1. ἀδελφοὶ _____ οἴκους.

It means _____

δοῦλε - δούλοις

2. _____, διδάσκεις υἱοὺς ἀνθρώπων.

It means _____

ἀγγέλους - ἄγγελος

3. γινώσκω ἀποστόλους καὶ _____.

It means _____

ἀκούω - ἀκούουσιν

4. ἀπόστολοι _____ ἄνθρωπον.

It means _____

νόμου - νόμον

5. γράφομεν λόγους _____.

It means _____

δοῦλος - δοῦλοι

6. _____ λαμβάνουσιν οἶκον ἀδελφοῦ.

It means _____

λέγουσι - λέγουσιν

7. ἄνθρωποι _____ λόγον ἀγγέλῳ.

It means _____

☐ Flashcards

28

Greek Workbook - Level 4
Copyright © 1995 by Karen Mohs

LET'S PRACTICE

Circle the correct words.

servants	to a man	of apostles
δοῦλοι	ἄνθρωπον	ἀποστόλου
δούλων	ἀνθρώπῳ	ἀποστόλους
δούλοις	ἀνθρώπων	ἀποστόλων
of a law	**you know**	**a word**
νόμος	γινώσκετε	λόγοι
νόμου	γινώσκει	λόγους
νόμῳ	γινώσκομεν	λόγον
for men	**to brothers**	**to a law**
ἀνθρώποις	ἀδελφῷ	νόμους
ἀνθρώπου	ἀδελφοῖς	νόμον
ἄνθρωπε	ἀδελφοῦ	νόμῳ
they hear	**of an angel**	**for a word**
ἀκούουσι	ἀγγέλων	λόγοις
ἀκούεις	ἄγγελον	λόγῳ
ἀκούει	ἀγγέλου	λόγου
for a house	**to sons**	**a man**
οἴκου	υἱοῖς	ἀνθρώπους
οἴκοις	υἱούς	ἄνθρωπος
οἴκῳ	υἱῷ	ἄνθρωποι
apostles	**for angels**	**brothers**
ἀπόστολοι	ἄγγελοι	ἀδελφός
ἀπόστολον	ἀγγέλοις	ἀδελφῶν
ἀποστόλοις	ἀγγέλῳ	ἀδελφούς

☐ Flashcards

Greek Workbook - Level 4
Copyright © 1995 by Karen Mohs

DO YOU REMEMBER?

Nouns ending in ον are neuter nouns.

δῶρον means **a gift**.

If we want to write about *more than one* gift, we write
δῶρα

Neuter nouns, like δῶρον and δῶρα, have the same spelling for subjects, direct objects, and words of direct address.

Circle the meanings of the neuter nouns.

ἱερόν	gifts	a door	a temple
δῶρον	a temple	a gift	of a gift
δώρῳ	to (or for) a gift	of a gift	temples
ἱεροῦ	gifts	of a temple	of temples
δῶρα	temples	a gift	gifts
ἱερά	gifts	temples	of gifts
ἱερῷ	to (or for) temples	of gifts	to (or for) a temple
δώροις	to (or for) gifts	gifts	of gifts

Choose the correct form, ἱερόν or ἱερά. Write it in the blank.

_____ 1. **A temple** has men.　　_____ 4. A servant sees **temples**.

_____ 2. **Temples** have laws.　　_____ 5. **Temple**, you have laws.

_____ 3. A son sees **a temple**.　　_____ 6. **Temples**, you teach men.

☐ Flashcards - (Add the new cards.)

30

Greek Workbook - Level 4
Copyright © 1995 by Karen Mohs

LET'S PRACTICE

Choose the best words for the sentences below. Put them in the blanks.
Write what the sentences mean.

λέγομεν	δῶρον	ἀποστόλων

1. ἄνθρωπος βλέπει οἴκους _____.

   It means _____

2. _____ λόγους υἱοῖς δούλων.

   It means _____

3. ἀδελφοὶ λαμβάνουσι _____.

   It means _____

δῶρα	ἄγγελοι	γράφει

1. ἀπόστολος _____ νόμους ἀνθρώποις.

   It means _____

2. υἱέ, λαμβάνεις _____ καὶ βλέπεις ἀδελφούς.

   It means _____

3. _____ γινώσκουσιν ἀνθρώπους καὶ υἱὸν δούλου.

   It means _____

☐ Flashcards

Greek Workbook - Level 4
Copyright © 1995 by Karen Mohs

31

LET'S PRACTICE

Read these Greek sentences. Write what they mean.

1. δοῦλοι ἔχουσιν υἱοὺς καὶ γινώσκουσιν ἀδελφοὺς ἀποστόλων.

    It means _____

2. ἔχετε δῶρα ἀνθρώποις καὶ ἀδελφοῖς δούλων.

    It means _____

3. ἄνθρωπε, βλέπομεν οἴκους καὶ ἱερὰ ἀνθρώπων.

    It means _____

4. διδάσκεις λόγους υἱῷ ἀδελφοῦ καὶ ἀδελφῷ υἱοῦ.

    It means _____

5. ἄγγελος λαμβάνει δῶρον καὶ βλέπει οἶκον.

    It means _____

6. ἄνθρωπος καὶ ἀδελφὸς λέγουσι νόμους υἱοῖς.

    It means _____

7. γινώσκω ἱερὸν καὶ ἀκούω ἀγγέλους καὶ δούλους.

    It means _____

8. γράφομεν νόμον ἀνθρώπῳ καὶ δούλῳ ἀνθρώπου.

    It means _____

9. ἀπόστολοι καὶ ἄγγελοι βλέπουσιν οἴκους ἀδελφῶν καὶ υἱῶν.

    It means _____

10. δοῦλος καὶ ἀπόστολος ἔχουσι λόγον καὶ νόμον.

    It means _____

☐ Flashcards

32

Greek Workbook - Level 4
Copyright © 1995 by Karen Mohs

Lesson 6

ὁ κύριος

means

the Lord, the lord

It sounds like ho **koo**-ree-os.

Write the Greek word that means **the Lord** or **the lord**.

Circle the words that mean the same as the first words in the rows.

the apostle	ὁ λόγος	ὁ ἀπόστολος	τὸ δῶρον
the Lord	ὁ κύριος	ὁ ἄγγελος	τὸ ἱερόν
I teach	λέγω	γράφω	διδάσκω
the angel	ὁ υἱός	ὁ ἄγγελος	ὁ ἄνθρωπος
I have	ἔχω	λαμβάνω	γινώσκω
the gift	ὁ ἀδελφός	τὸ δῶρον	τὸ ἱερόν
the man	ὁ υἱός	ὁ ἀπόστολος	ὁ ἄνθρωπος
the brother	ὁ δοῦλος	ὁ ἀδελφός	ὁ ἄγγελος
I hear	λέγω	λαμβάνω	ἀκούω
the temple	τὸ ἱερόν	ὁ νόμος	ὁ οἶκος
I see	διδάσκω	βλέπω	γράφω
the house	ὁ νόμος	ὁ λόγος	ὁ οἶκος

☐ Flashcards - (Add the new card.)

Greek Workbook - Level 4
Copyright © 1995 by Karen Mohs

33

LET'S PRACTICE

Write the Greek word that means **the Lord** or **the lord**.

Write the Greek words.

the gift

the lord

the temple

the angel

the law

☐ Flashcards

λύω

means

I loose,* I destroy

It sounds like **loo**-o.

Write the Greek word that means **I loose** or **I destroy**.

Match the words to their meanings.

ὁ κύριος	I destroy
λαμβάνω	the son
τὸ δῶρον	the gift
ὁ υἱός	I take
λύω	the Lord
γράφω	I say
λέγω	I write
τὸ ἱερόν	the temple
ὁ οἶκος	the house
ὁ ἄγγελος	the law
ἔχω	the angel
ὁ νόμος	I have
διδάσκω	I hear
ἀκούω	I teach

*Since *I loose* is not in common use today, your student may prefer translating λύω with the words, *I destroy*.

☐ Flashcards - (Add the new card.)

Greek Workbook - Level 4
Copyright © 1995 by Karen Mohs

35

LET'S PRACTICE

Write the Greek word that means **I loose** or **I destroy**.

Write the Greek words.

I take

I destroy

I hear

I loose

I have

☐ Flashcards

ὁ θεός

means

God, the god

It sounds like ho theh-**os**.

Write the Greek word that means **God** or **the god**.

Circle the correct words.

I see	the man	I destroy
ἀκούω	ὁ ἄνθρωπος	λαμβάνω
βλέπω	ὁ δοῦλος	ἔχω
λέγω	ὁ υἱός	λύω
the brother	the god	the apostle
ὁ οἶκος	ὁ θεός	ὁ λόγος
ὁ ἀδελφός	ὁ ἄγγελος	ὁ ἀπόστολος
ὁ ἄνθρωπος	τὸ δῶρον	τὸ ἱερόν
the lord	I know	I write
ὁ ἄγγελος	λύω	διδάσκω
ὁ κύριος	βλέπω	γράφω
ὁ νόμος	γινώσκω	ἔχω

☐ Flashcards - (Add the new card.)

Greek Workbook - Level 4
Copyright © 1995 by Karen Mohs

LET'S PRACTICE

Write the Greek word that means **God** or **the god**.

Write the Greek words.

the word

the son

the servant

the house

God

☐ Flashcards

Lesson 7

$$\overline{\dot{\epsilon}\gamma\epsilon\acute{\iota}\rho\omega}$$

means

I raise up

It sounds like e-**gay**-ro.

Write the Greek word that means **I raise up**.

Write the meanings of the following Greek words.

τὸ δῶρον _____

ὁ θεός _____

λέγω _____

ἐγείρω _____

διδάσκω _____

ἔχω _____

ὁ κύριος _____

ὁ οἶκος _____

ἀκούω _____

ὁ υἱός _____

λύω _____

ὁ νόμος _____

ὁ ἄγγελος _____

τὸ ἱερόν _____

λαμβάνω _____

☐ Flashcards - (Add the new card.)

Greek Workbook - Level 4
Copyright © 1995 by Karen Mohs

39

LET'S PRACTICE

Write the Greek word that means **I raise up**.

Write the Greek words.

I loose

I teach

I say

I raise up

I write

☐ Flashcards

40

ὁ θάνατος

means

the death

It sounds like ho **tha**-na-tos.

Write the Greek word that means **the death**.

_____

- -

_____

Match the Greek words to their meanings.

_____	1. ὁ υἱός	a.	the Lord
_____	2. ὁ κύριος	b.	the son
_____	3. ὁ δοῦλος	c.	the house
_____	4. ὁ οἶκος	d.	the slave
_____	5. ὁ θάνατος	e.	God
_____	6. ὁ λόγος	f.	the death
_____	7. ὁ θεός	g.	the word
_____	8. γινώσκω	h.	I see
_____	9. ἐγείρω	i.	I know
_____	10. διδάσκω	j.	I raise up
_____	11. βλέπω	k.	I teach
_____	12. λύω	l.	I destroy
_____	13. λέγω	m.	I write
_____	14. γράφω	n.	I say

☐ Flashcards - (Add the new card.)

Greek Workbook - Level 4
Copyright © 1995 by Karen Mohs

41

LET'S PRACTICE

Write the Greek word that means **the death**.

Write the Greek words.

the lord

the apostle

the god

the brother

the death

☐ Flashcards

means

I lead

It sounds like **a**-go.

Write the Greek word that means **I lead**.

Circle the correct words.

the Lord	ὁ κύριος ὁ υἱός ὁ ἀδελφός	I destroy	διδάσκω λύω ἄγω
I lead	βλέπω ἄγω γινώσκω	God	ὁ νόμος ὁ λόγος ὁ θεός
the death	ὁ ἄγγελος ὁ οἶκος ὁ θάνατος	the temple	τὸ ἱερόν τὸ δῶρον ὁ δοῦλος
I take	ἀκούω λέγω λαμβάνω	I raise up	γράφω ἔχω ἐγείρω

☐ Flashcards - (Add the new card.)

LET'S PRACTICE

Write the Greek word that means **I lead**.

Write the Greek words.

I lead

I know

I raise up

I see

I loose

☐ Flashcards

44

Greek Workbook - Level 4
Copyright © 1995 by Karen Mohs

Lesson 8

means

the world

It sounds like ho **ko**-smos.

Write the Greek word that means **the world**.

Circle the correct words.

I raise up	the lord	I lead
ἐγείρω	τὸ δῶρον	βλέπω
γινώσκω	τὸ ἱερόν	ἄγω
ἀκούω	ὁ κύριος	ἔχω
the god	the world	I teach
ὁ ἀπόστολος	ὁ λόγος	λέγω
ὁ θεός	ὁ κόσμος	λαμβάνω
ὁ ἀδελφός	ὁ δοῦλος	διδάσκω
the death	the angel	I destroy
ὁ οἶκος	ὁ ἄγγελος	γράφω
ὁ νόμος	ὁ ἄνθρωπος	λύω
ὁ θάνατος	ὁ υἱός	ἄγω

☐ Flashcards - (Add the new card.)

LET'S PRACTICE

Write the Greek word that means **the world**.

Write the Greek words.

the death

the man

the temple

the world

God

☐ Flashcards

LET'S PRACTICE

The words ending in **os** are masculine. Write these words.

the son _____

the servant _____

the angel _____

the brother _____

the death _____

the house _____

the world _____

the man _____

the Lord _____

the law _____

the word _____

God _____

the apostle _____

The words ending in **ov** are neuter. Write these words.

the gift _____

the temple _____

☐ Flashcards

Greek Workbook - Level 4
Copyright © 1995 by Karen Mohs

PUZZLE TIME

Think of the meanings of the Greek words. Write the English words on the puzzle below.

across

1. λέγω means I _____
2. ἄγγελος means an _____
6. οἶκος means a _____
9. κόσμος means a _____
10. ἀπόστολος means an _____
12. γινώσκω means I _____
15. ἐγείρω means I _____ up
17. κύριος means a _____
18. ἱερόν means a _____
20. θάνατος means a _____
22. ἀδελφός means a _____
23. διδάσκω means I _____

down

1. βλέπω means I _____
3. δῶρον means a _____
4. θεός means a _____
5. δοῦλος means a _____
7. υἱός means a _____
8. λύω means I _____
9. λόγος means a _____
11. ἄγω means I _____
13. γράφω means I _____
14. ἀκούω means I _____
16. νόμος means a _____
18. λαμβάνω means I _____
19. ἄνθρωπος means a _____
21. ἔχω means I _____

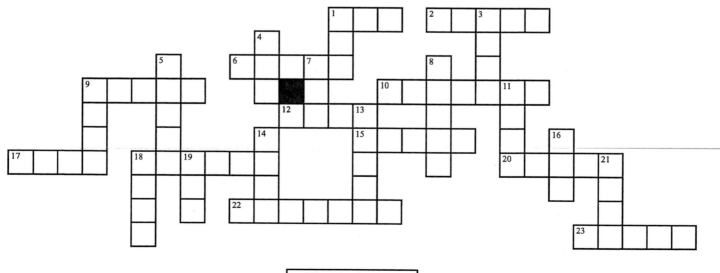

☐ Flashcards

48

Greek Workbook - Level 4
Copyright © 1995 by Karen Mohs

Lesson 9

THE SINGULAR MASCULINE ARTICLE

In English, we can put the definite article ("the") in front of any noun.
In Greek, there is a special article for each case of noun.

Singular

Nominative   ἀδελφός means **a brother.**

           ὁ ἀδελφός means *the* **brother.**

Genitive   ἀδελφοῦ means **of a brother.**

      τοῦ ἀδελφοῦ means **of** *the* **brother.**

Dative   ἀδελφῷ means **to (or for) a brother.**

       τῷ ἀδελφῷ means **to (or for)** *the* **brother.**

Accusative   ἀδελφόν means **a brother.**

     τὸν ἀδελφόν means *the* **brother.**

There is no article for ἀδελφέ, the vocative case used for direct address.

Match the articles to their words and the words to their meanings.

τὸν	νόμῳ	the angel
ὁ	υἱόν	to the law
τῷ	ἄγγελος	the son
τὸν	υἱοῦ	the house
τοῦ	οἶκον	for the word
τῷ	δοῦλος	of the son
ὁ	λόγῳ	the servant
τὸν	ἀγγέλῳ	of the man
τοῦ	ἀνθρώπου	to the angel
τῷ	ἀπόστολον	the apostle

☐ Flashcards

Greek Workbook - Level 4
Copyright © 1995 by Karen Mohs

LET'S PRACTICE

Write the correct articles before the words. Write the meanings.

1. _____ ἀδελφῷ   It means _____

2. _____ νόμος   It means _____

3. _____ θάνατον   It means _____

4. _____ υἱόν   It means _____

5. _____ θεοῦ   It means _____

6. _____ οἶκον   It means _____

7. _____ κόσμῳ   It means _____

8. _____ ἀγγέλου   It means _____

9. _____ δοῦλον   It means _____

10. _____ κύριος   It means _____

☐ Flashcards

THE PLURAL MASCULINE ARTICLE

We have learned the ways to write "the" for the singular Greek nouns. There is also a special definite article for each plural Greek noun.

Plural

Nominative   ἀδελφοί means **brothers.**

                 οἱ ἀδελφοί means *the* **brothers.**

Genitive   ἀδελφῶν means **of brothers.**

                 τῶν ἀδελφῶν means **of** *the* **brothers.**

Dative   ἀδελφοῖς means **to (or for) brothers.**

                 τοῖς ἀδελφοῖς means **to (or for)** *the* **brothers.**

Accusative   ἀδελφούς means **brothers.**

                 τοὺς ἀδελφούς means *the* **brothers.**

Just as in the singular, there is no article for the plural vocative, the case of direct address.

Match the articles to their words and the words to their meanings.

τοὺς	κύριοι	the gods
τοῖς	θεούς	for the deaths
οἱ	θανάτοις	the lords

τοὺς	θεοί	the gods
οἱ	ἀδελφούς	the brothers
τῶν	κυρίοις	of the apostles
τοῖς	ἀποστόλων	to the lords

οἱ	θεοῖς	of the lords
τῶν	κυρίων	the words
τοῖς	λόγοι	for the gods

☐ Flashcards

Greek Workbook - Level 4
Copyright © 1995 by Karen Mohs

LET'S PRACTICE

Write the correct articles before the words. Write the meanings.

1. _____ οἴκων   It means _____

2. _____ ἀγγέλοις   It means _____

3. _____ ἄνθρωποι   It means _____

4. _____ υἱός   It means _____

5. _____ ἀδελφῶν   It means _____

6. _____ ἄγγελοι   It means _____

7. _____ νόμους   It means _____

8. _____ δούλῳ   It means _____

9. _____ θεοί   It means _____

10. _____ λόγου   It means _____

☐ Flashcards

LET'S PRACTICE

Circle the correct words. Write what the sentences mean.

1. (οἱ, ὁ) κύριος ἐγείρει (τοὺς, τοῦ) υἱοὺς (τοῦ, τῶν) ἀδελφοῦ.

   It means _____

2. (ὁ, τὸν) ἄνθρωπος ἀκούει (τοῖς, τοὺς) λόγους τοῦ κυρίου.

   It means _____

3. (ὁ, τῷ) κόσμος γινώσκει θάνατον, καὶ βλέπομεν τὸν θεόν.

   It means _____

4. κύριε, διδάσκεις (τὸν, ὁ) λόγον (τὸν, τοῦ) θεοῦ.

   It means _____

5. (οἱ, ὁ) δοῦλοι βλέπουσι (τοὺς, τὸν) οἴκους (τοῖς, τοῦ) κόσμου.

   It means _____

6. (τοῦ, οἱ) κύριοι θανάτου λαμβάνουσι (τοὺς, τὸν) ἄνθρωπον.

   It means _____

7. ἀδελφοί, βλέπετε (οἱ, τοὺς) ἀγγέλους καὶ λαμβάνετε τὸν κόσμον.

   It means _____

8. ἄγω (τοὺς, οἱ) ἀποστόλους καὶ λύω (τοὺς, τοῦ) δούλους.

   It means _____

9. (οἱ, ὁ) ἀδελφοὶ ἔχουσι (τὸν, τοὺς) οἶκον (τῷ, τῶν) δούλων.

   It means _____

10. γράφομεν νόμον (τῶν, τοῖς) δούλοις (τῶν, τοῖς) υἱῶν.

    It means _____

☐ Flashcards

Greek Workbook - Level 4
Copyright © 1995 by Karen Mohs

53

LET'S PRACTICE

Write the correct Greek articles in the sentences. Write what they mean.
Articles may be used more than once or not at all.

1. _____ ἀπόστολος γράφει λόγον _____ ἀδελφοῖς.

   It means _____

2. _____ λόγος _____ νόμου ἄγει ἀνθρώπους.

   It means _____

3. _____ ἄγγελος ἔχει δῶρον _____ κυρίῳ.

   It means _____

ὁ
τοῦ
τῷ
τὸν
οἱ
τῶν
τοῖς
τοὺς

---

1. θεέ, διδάσκεις _____ ἀδελφὸν _____ δούλου.

   It means _____

2. _____ ἀδελφὸς βλέπει ἱερὸν _____ ἀνθρώπων.

   It means _____

3. _____ ἀπόστολοι γινώσκουσι _____ ἀγγέλους.

   It means _____

ὁ
τοῦ
τῷ
τὸν
οἱ
τῶν
τοῖς
τοὺς

☐ Flashcards

54

Greek Workbook - Level 4
Copyright © 1995 by Karen Mohs

Lesson 10

THE NEUTER ARTICLE

Some neuter nouns (*subjects* and *direct objects*)
have their own special articles.

Singular
Nominative and accusative   δῶρον means **a gift.**

                           τὸ δῶρον means *the* **gift.**

Plural
Nominative and accusative   δῶρα means **gifts.**

                           τὰ δῶρα means *the* **gifts.**

Neuter nouns, like masculine nouns, have no articles for
singular or plural vocative words, the case of direct address.

Match the articles to their words and the words to their meanings.

τὸ	λόγων	the gift
τὰ	ἱερῷ	the temples
ὁ	δῶρον	the god
τῶν	ἱερά	of the words
τῷ	θεός	to the temple
τὸ	ἱερόν	the gifts
οἱ	δῶρα	the temple
τὰ	υἱοί	for the gift
τῷ	δώρῳ	the sons
τὸ	δώροις	the temple
τοῖς	ἱερόν	for the gifts
τοῦ	ἱεροῦ	of the angels
τῶν	θανάτῳ	of the temple
τῷ	ἀγγέλων	to the death

☐ Flashcards

Greek Workbook - Level 4
Copyright © 1995 by Karen Mohs

55

LET'S PRACTICE

Write the correct articles before the words. Write the meanings.

1. _____ ἀνθρώπῳ   It means _____

2. _____ λόγοις   It means _____

3. _____ υἱῷ   It means _____

4. _____ ἄγγελον   It means _____

5. _____ ἀνθρώποις   It means _____

6. _____ οἴκῳ   It means _____

7. _____ ἀποστόλοις   It means _____

8. _____ κύριον   It means _____

9. _____ θεῷ   It means _____

10. _____ υἱοῖς   It means _____

☐ Flashcards

LET'S PRACTICE

Write the words on the right under the correct articles.

τοῖς	τὸν	οἱ

τοῦ	ὁ	τοὺς

τῶν	τῷ	τὰ

τὸ

θεοῖς
οἶκος
ἀδελφοί
ἀγγέλων
λόγοις
κόσμῳ
νόμους
υἱοῦ
θεόν
δῶρα
ἄγγελοι
ἱερά
οἴκοις
ἀνθρώπων
θάνατος
ἀποστόλους
οἴκου
λόγῳ
ἱερόν
θάνατον
κυρίῳ
ἀνθρώπους
δοῦλοι
κυρίων
θεός
ἀποστόλου
νόμον

☐ Flashcards

Greek Workbook - Level 4
Copyright © 1995 by Karen Mohs

57

LET'S PRACTICE

Choose the correct articles for these sentences. Write the meanings.

ὁ τῷ τοῖς τοὺς	1. _____ ἄνθρωπος διδάσκει _____ υἱούς. It means _____
τῶν τὸν οἱ τὸ	2. βλέπω _____ ἱερὸν _____ ἀνθρώπων. It means _____
τοὺς τῶν τοῦ τῷ	3. γινώσκετε _____ λόγους _____ νόμου. It means _____
ὁ τοῖς τοὺς τὸ	4. ἔχομεν _____ δῶρον _____ ἀποστόλοις. It means _____
τῶν τὸν τῷ τοῦ	5. λέγεις _____ λόγον _____ ἀγγέλῳ. It means _____
τοὺς ὁ οἱ τῷ	6. _____ ἄγγελοι ἀκούουσι _____ ἀδελφούς. It means _____
τοὺς οἱ τοῖς τοῦ	7. _____ ἄνθρωποι λύουσι _____ δούλους. It means _____
τὸν τοὺς τῶν τῷ	8. γράφει _____ νόμους _____ κόσμῳ. It means _____

☐ Flashcards

58

Greek Workbook - Level 4
Copyright © 1995 by Karen Mohs

Lesson 11

ὁ λίθος

means

the stone

It sounds like ho **lee**-thos.*

Write the Greek word that means **the stone**.

_____

Write the meanings of the following Greek words.

βλέπω _____

ὁ ἀδελφός _____

ὁ κόσμος _____

ὁ ἀπόστολος _____

τὸ δῶρον _____

γράφω _____

ὁ λίθος _____

ἄγω _____

γινώσκω _____

ὁ ἄνθρωπος _____

ὁ κύριος _____

ὁ λόγος _____

τὸ ἱερόν _____

ὁ θάνατος _____

ὁ δοῦλος _____

*Although this iota appears long because of its pronunciation, think of it as a short vowel.

☐ Flashcards - (Add the new card.)

Greek Workbook - Level 4
Copyright © 1995 by Karen Mohs

LET'S PRACTICE

Write the Greek word that means **the stone**.

Write the Greek words.

the Lord

the stone

the death

the world

the temple

☐ Flashcards

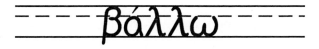

means

I throw, I cast, I put

It sounds like **bal**-lo.

Write the Greek word that means **I throw** or **I cast** or **I put**.

Match the words to their meanings.

ὁ κόσμος	the death
ἐγείρω	the stone
ὁ θάνατος	the world
ὁ λίθος	I raise up
ἄγω	I lead
γινώσκω	I know
ὁ θεός	the temple
βλέπω	God
τὸ ἱερόν	I see
ὁ κύριος	I throw
βάλλω	the lord
λαμβάνω	I destroy
τὸ δῶρον	the gift
λύω	I take

☐ Flashcards - (Add the new card.)

LET'S PRACTICE

Write the Greek word that means **I throw** or **I cast** or **I put**.

Write the Greek words.

I have

I lead

I hear

I loose

I put

□ Flashcards

62

ὁ οὐρανός

means

the heaven

It sounds like ho oo-ra-**nos**.

Write the Greek word that means **the heaven**.

Match the Greek words to their meanings.

_____ 1. ὁ κόσμος   a. the heaven

_____ 2. ὁ λίθος   b. the angel

_____ 3. ὁ οὐρανός   c. the son

_____ 4. ὁ ἄγγελος   d. the temple

_____ 5. τὸ ἱερόν   e. the gift

_____ 6. ὁ υἱός   f. the world

_____ 7. τὸ δῶρον   g. the stone

_____ 8. λαμβάνω   h. I hear

_____ 9. ἄγω   i. I destroy

_____ 10. ἀκούω   j. I have

_____ 11. ἐγείρω   k. I take

_____ 12. ἔχω   l. I cast

_____ 13. βάλλω   m. I lead

_____ 14. λύω   n. I raise up

☐ Flashcards - (Add the new card.)

LET'S PRACTICE

Write the Greek word that means **the heaven**.

Write the Greek words.

the stone

the angel

the gift

the heaven

the world

☐ Flashcards

64

Greek Workbook - Level 4
Copyright © 1995 by Karen Mohs

Lesson 12

means

I remain

It sounds like **me**-no.

Write the Greek word that means **I remain**.

Circle the correct words.

the stone	I lead	I remain
ὁ κύριος	λέγω	ἔχω
ὁ λίθος	λύω	μένω
ὁ λόγος	ἄγω	ἀκούω
the death	the heaven	the angel
τὸ ἱερόν	ὁ οὐρανός	τὸ δῶρον
ὁ θάνατος	ὁ οἶκος	ὁ δοῦλος
ὁ θεός	ὁ ἄνθρωπος	ὁ ἄγγελος
I throw	the world	I raise up
βλέπω	ὁ κόσμος	διδάσκω
λαμβάνω	ὁ νόμος	ἐγείρω
βάλλω	ὁ υἱός	γράφω

☐ Flashcards - (Add the new card.)

LET'S PRACTICE

Write the Greek word that means **I remain**.

Write the Greek words.

I remain

I take

I put

I raise up

I lead

☐ Flashcards

66

Greek Workbook - Level 4
Copyright © 1995 by Karen Mohs

ΤÒ ΤΈΚΝΟΝ

means

the child

It sounds like to **te**-knon.

Write the Greek word that means **the child**.

_____

_ _

_____

Circle the correct words.

I lead	ἔχω ἄγω λύω	the stone	ὁ λίθος τὸ ἱερόν ὁ οἶκος
the heaven	ὁ οὐρανός ὁ υἱός ὁ ἄγγελος	the child	τὸ δῶρον ὁ λόγος τὸ τέκνον
I put	ἐγείρω ἀκούω βάλλω	the death	ὁ θάνατος ὁ θεός ὁ νόμος
the world	ὁ κύριος ὁ κόσμος ὁ δοῦλος	I remain	μένω λέγω βλέπω

☐ Flashcards - (Add the new card.)

Greek Workbook - Level 4
Copyright © 1995 by Karen Mohs

LET'S PRACTICE

Write the Greek word that means **the child**.

Write the Greek words.

the heaven

the law

the child

the stone

the house

☐ Flashcards

68

πέμπω

means

I send

It sounds like **pem**-po.

Write the Greek word that means **I send**.

_____

– –

Write the meanings of the following Greek words.

ὁ λίθος _____

λύω _____

μένω _____

ὁ κύριος _____

ὁ κόσμος _____

ὁ θάνατος _____

ὁ οὐρανός _____

τὸ ἱερόν _____

βάλλω _____

τὸ δῶρον _____

ἐγείρω _____

πέμπω _____

ὁ θεός _____

ἄγω _____

τὸ τέκνον _____

☐ Flashcards - (Add the new card.)

Greek Workbook - Level 4
Copyright © 1995 by Karen Mohs

69

LET'S PRACTICE

Write the Greek word that means **I send**.

Write the Greek words.

I remain

I cast

I say

I send

I teach

☐ Flashcards

Lesson 13

ὁ ΤΌΠΟS

means

the place

It sounds like ho **to**-pos.

Write the Greek word that means **the place**.

Circle the words that mean the same as the first words in the rows.

I raise up	λαμβάνω	ἐγείρω	μένω
the death	ὁ θάνατος	ὁ νόμος	ὁ δοῦλος
I loose	λέγω	γινώσκω	λύω
the place	ὁ τόπος	ὁ θεός	ὁ λόγος
I send	βλέπω	πέμπω	γράφω
the world	ὁ κύριος	ὁ κόσμος	ὁ ἀδελφός
the heaven	ὁ οἶκος	τὸ ἱερόν	ὁ οὐρανός
I lead	ἔχω	ἄγω	λύω
I throw	βάλλω	πέμπω	διδάσκω
the child	ὁ ἄγγελος	τὸ τέκνον	τὸ δῶρον
the stone	ὁ λίθος	ὁ ἀπόστολος	ὁ υἱός
I remain	ἀκούω	βάλλω	μένω

☐ Flashcards - (Add the new card.)

Greek Workbook - Level 4
Copyright © 1995 by Karen Mohs

71

LET'S PRACTICE

Write the Greek word that means **the place**.

Write the Greek words.

the child

the gift

the stone

the place

the heaven

☐ Flashcards

means

I bear, I bring

It sounds like **fe**-ro.

Write the Greek word that means **I bear** or **I bring**.

Match the words to their meanings.

ὁ κύριος	I bear
ὁ κόσμος	the god
φέρω	I destroy
ὁ θεός	the world
λύω	the lord
τὸ τέκνον	I put
βάλλω	the child
ὁ θάνατος	the death
πέμπω	I send
ἄγω	the heaven
ὁ οὐρανός	the place
μένω	I lead
ὁ τόπος	the stone
ὁ λίθος	I remain

☐ Flashcards - (Add the new card.)

LET'S PRACTICE

Write the Greek word that means **I bear** or **I bring**.

Write the Greek words.

I remain

I write

I send

I throw

I bring

☐ Flashcards

LET'S PRACTICE

Write the Greek words.

I have _____

I raise up _____

I bear _____

I say _____

I hear _____

I remain _____

I loose _____

the child _____

I put _____

the heaven _____

I take _____

I lead _____

the place _____

the stone _____

the world _____

the law _____

☐ Flashcards

Greek Workbook - Level 4
Copyright © 1995 by Karen Mohs

75

PUZZLE TIME

Unscramble the following Greek words. Write them in the sentences below.
Then write what the sentences mean.

κμοόσυ _____   όογλsυ _____

άλοοόπσsτυ _____   άγρφω _____

αδρῶ _____   έκννοτ _____

1. τὸ _____ τοῦ ἀδελφοῦ φέρει τὰ _____ .

   It means _____

2. οἱ δοῦλοι τοῦ _____ βάλλουσι τοὺς λίθους.

   It means _____

3. πέμπω τὰ δῶρα καὶ λέγω τοὺς _____ .

   It means _____

4. _____ τοὺς λόγους τοῦ θεοῦ τοῖς τέκνοις.

   It means _____

5. οἱ ἄγγελοι ἄγουσι τοὺς _____ καὶ τοὺς υἱούς.

   It means _____

☐ Flashcards

76

Greek Workbook - Level 4
Copyright © 1995 by Karen Mohs

Lesson 14

VOWELS

Short Vowels:		Long Vowels:	
α	**a** in *father*	α	**a** in *father*, but held longer
ε	**e** in *get*	η	**a** in *late*
ο	**o** in *obey*	ω	**o** in *note*
ι	**i** in *pit*	ι	**ee** in *feet*
υ	**oo** in *good*	υ	**oo** in *good*, but held longer

Match the Greek vowels to their sounds.

(long) υ   **o** in *note*

(long) α   **oo** in *good*, but held longer

ω   **e** in *get*

(short) υ   **a** in *father*, but held longer

ε   **oo** in *good*

(short) ι   **a** in *father*

η   **ee** in *feet*

(long) ι   **a** in *late*

(short) α   **i** in *pit*

(long) α   **oo** in *good*

(short) υ   **a** in *father*, but held longer

ο   **o** in *obey*

ω   **e** in *get*

ε   **o** in *note*

☐ Flashcards - (Add the new cards.)

Greek Workbook - Level 4
Copyright © 1995 by Karen Mohs

DIPHTHONGS & IOTA SUBSCRIPTS

The most common Greek diphthongs are as follows:

αι	**ai** in *aisle*
ει	**a** in *fate* (same sound as η)
οι	**oi** in *oil*
αυ	**ow** in *cow*
ευ	**eu** in *feud*
ου	**oo** in *food*
υι	**uee** in *queen*

A diphthong combines two vowels into one syllable.
For example, the **oi** in our English word **boil** is a diphthong.

Match the Greek diphthongs to their sounds.

οι	**ai** in *aisle*	ευ	**uee** in *queen*
ου	**oo** in *food*	υι	**a** in *fate*
αι	**oi** in *oil*	ει	**eu** in *feud*
αυ	**ow** in *cow*		

When an iota (ι) follows certain long vowels (α, η, ω), it is written below the letter instead of after it (ᾳ, ῃ, ῳ). This is called an **iota subscript**. These diphthongs sound the same as the long vowels alone.

Write three long vowels with their iota subscripts: _____ . _____ . _____ .

☐ Flashcards - (Add the new cards.)

Lesson 15

BREATHINGS

If a vowel or a diphthong begins a word, it always has a **breathing mark** positioned directly above it. (On a diphthong, the breathing mark is on the second vowel.)

Breathing marks come in two shapes.

1. The rough breathing mark (ʽ)
   With this mark, read the word with an h-sound before the first vowel.

2. The smooth breathing mark (ʼ)
   With this mark, there is no h-sound.

For example:

ἐν sounds like *en*.
ἑν sounds like *hen*.

Whenever the consonant ρ begins a word, it has a rough breathing mark.

Circle the words with the correct breathing marks.

ὁ	ὀ	It sounds like **ho**.
ἅγιος	ἀγιος	It sounds like **hag**-ee-os.
ἱερόν	ἰερόν	It sounds like hee-er-**on**.
ἑπτά	ἐπτά	It sounds like hep-**tah**.
ἑξ	ἐξ	It sounds like **ex**.
ἅγω	ἀγω	It sounds like **ag**-o.
ρακά	ῥακά	It sounds like rhak-**ah**.
εἱς	εἰς	It sounds like **ace**.
οἱ	οἰ	It sounds like **hoy**.

☐ Flashcards - (Add the new card.)

Greek Workbook - Level 4
Copyright © 1995 by Karen Mohs

79

ACCENTS

The Greek language has three types of accents.*

1. The acute accent (´)
2. The circumflex accent (ˆ)
3. The grave accent (`)

An accent only stands over vowels. If the vowel is part of a diphthong, the accent stands over the second vowel of the pair. If a breathing mark and an acute accent stand over the same vowel, the breathing mark is always first. (ἄγω) If a breathing mark and a circumflex stand over the same vowel, the circumflex is placed over the breathing mark. (οἶκος)

Accents show which syllable to stress** when you pronounce a word.

Cross out the words that are not accented correctly.

Remember!			
SHORT VOWELS	γράμμα	μηδείς	πίστις
α a in *father*	ἵνα	σάρξ	ὄχλος
ε e in *get*	μείζων	ἔβαλον	εἶπον
o o in *obey*	σπείρω	ἤ	τηρέω
ι i in *pit*	εἶδον	ποῖος	εἶς
υ oo in *good*	ζάω	οὖν	γυνή
LONG VOWELS	ἤχθη	ἰδών	ὤφθην
α a in *father*, held longer	οἶδα	οὖσα	ὄρος
η a in *late*	ἰδού	πούς	χάρις
ω o in *note*	ἔσομαι	χέιρ	πλείων
ι ee in *feet*			
υ oo in *good*, held longer			
DIPHTHONGS			
αι οι ου			
ει αυ υι			
ευ			

*Accents are difficult to learn. Accenting rules have been included to help the student understand why Greek accents change from syllable to syllable within the same word. These rules should be carefully learned only by those who plan to pursue in depth their study of Greek beyond this series. For most students, it is sufficient to read the rules and try to apply them to the exercises. Students should not be penalized for incorrect accent placement.

**In ancient times, the three accents were used to show musical pitch, not stress. Since today we cannot know the musical pitch used in those ancient times, we use the accents simply for stress.

☐ Flashcards - (Add the new card.)

80

Greek Workbook - Level 4
Copyright © 1995 by Karen Mohs

Lesson 16

NAMES OF SYLLABLES

Before we learn the **Rules of Accent**, we must know the names of the last three syllables of Greek words.

1. The last syllable is the **ultima**.
2. The syllable before the ultima is the **penult**.
3. The syllable before the penult is the **antepenult**.

ἀ   πό   στο   λος

antepenult   penult   ultima

Write *penult*, *ultima*, or *antepenult* on the lines beneath the syllables.

γι   νώ   σκου   σι

_____   _____   _____   _____

ἀν   θρώ   ποις

_____   _____   _____

λαμ   βά   νο   μεν

_____   _____   _____   _____

ἀ   κού   ου   σι

_____   _____   _____   _____

ἐ   γεί   ρε   τε

_____   _____   _____   _____

ἀ   πο   στό   λων

_____   _____   _____   _____

οὐ   ρα   νούς

_____   _____   _____

☐ Flashcards - (Add the new card.)

Greek Workbook - Level 4
Copyright © 1995 by Karen Mohs

81

LENGTH OF SYLLABLES

Long syllables:

    1. A syllable is long if it contains a long vowel.

        Example: πω in βλέπω is a long syllable.

    2. A syllable is long if it contains any diphthong (except αι or οι at the end of a word).

        Example: δοῦ in δοῦλος is a long syllable.

Short syllables:

    1. A syllable is short if it contains a short vowel.

        Example: γος in λόγος is a short syllable.

    2. A syllable is short if it contains αι or οι at the end of a word.

        Example: φοί in ἀδελφοί is a short syllable.

        BUT   φοῖς in ἀδελφοῖς is a long syllable because a letter (ς) comes after the οι.

If a syllable is long, write **long** on the line above it. If the syllable is short, write **short** on the line. For this exercise, if a vowel can be either long or short (α, ι, υ), assume it is short.

Remember!
SHORT VOWELS
α   a in *father*
ε   e in *get*
ο   o in *obey*
ι   i in *pit*
υ   oo in *good*
LONG VOWELS
α   a in *father*, held longer
η   a in *late*
ω   o in *note*
ι   ee in *feet*
υ   oo in *good*, held longer
DIPHTHONGS
αι   οι   ου
ει   αυ   υι
ευ

1.   νό   μους   5.   ἀ   κού   ει

2.   οἴ   κοις   6.   ἱ   ε   ρόν

3.   υἱ   οί   7.   οὐ   ρα   νῶν

4.   νό   μῳ   8.   ἀγ   γέ   λου

☐ Flashcards - (Add the new cards.)

LET'S PRACTICE

Circle the correct words.

1. In the word βλέπεις, the syllable βλέ is (short, long) and is called the (antepenult, penult, ultima).

2. In the word ἄνθρωπε, the syllable ἄν is (short, long) and is called the (antepenult, penult, ultima).

3. In the word λαμβάνει, the syllable βά is (short, long) and is called the (antepenult, penult, ultima).

4. In the word τέκνων, the syllable κνων is (short, long) and is called the (antepenult, penult, ultima).

5. In the word ἀκούεις, the syllable ἀ is (short, long) and is called the (antepenult, penult, ultima).

6. In the word υἱέ, the syllable υἱ is (short, long) and is called the (antepenult, penult, ultima).

7. In the word τόπῳ, the syllable πῳ is (short, long) and is called the (antepenult, penult, ultima).

8. In the word ἔχεις, the syllable χεις is (short, long) and is called the (antepenult, penult, ultima).

9. In the word λέγομεν, the syllable λέ is (short, long) and is called the (antepenult, penult, ultima).

10. In the word διδάσκω, the syllable δά is (short, long) and is called the (antepenult, penult, ultima).

☐ Flashcards

Greek Workbook - Level 4
Copyright © 1995 by Karen Mohs

LET'S PRACTICE

Write the words on the right under the correct headings. Words can be used more than once. For this exercise, if a vowel can be either long or short, assume it is short.

short ultima	long ultima	short penult

long penult	short antepenult	long antepenult

ἄγουσι

καί

ἀνθρώπους

γινώσκουσι

ἄγγελοι

οὐρανούς

τῶν

ἀκούομεν

λόγοις

κόσμῳ

Remember!

SHORT VOWELS
α   a in *father*
ε   e in *get*
ο   o in *obey*
ι   i in *pit*
υ   oo in *good*

LONG VOWELS
α   a in *father*, held longer
η   a in *late*
ω   o in *note*
ι   ee in *feet*
υ   oo in *good*, held longer

DIPHTHONGS
αι   οι   ου
ει   αυ   υι
  ευ

☐ Flashcards

84

Greek Workbook - Level 4
Copyright © 1995 by Karen Mohs

Lesson 17

GENERAL RULES OF ACCENT
The Acute Accent

1. The acute accent (´) can stand only on one of the last three syllables.

   Examples: ἄνθρωπος (The acute stands on the antepenult.)

   γινώσκει (The acute stands on the penult.)

   υἱός (The acute stands on the ultima.)

2. The acute accent (´) can stand on long or short syllables.

   Correct: τόπος (The acute stands on a short syllable.)

   Correct: γινώσκω (The acute stands on a long syllable.)

3. When the ultima is long, the acute accent (´) cannot stand on the antepenult.

   Incorrect: ἀπόστολων

   Correct: ἀποστόλων

4. When the ultima is short, the acute accent (´) cannot stand on a long penult.

   Incorrect: δώρον

   Correct: δῶρον

Cross out the words that are incorrectly accented. For this exercise, if a vowel can be either long or short, assume it is short.

ἄγγελων	θάνατος	ἀκούετε
φέρουσι	οἴκου	δοῦλοι
ἄνθρωπου	θάνατοις	γίνωσκουσι
λέγετε	ἄγγελους	λέγουσι
δώροις	βάλλομεν	ἔγειρει
~~γινώσκεις~~	~~ἀνθρώπῳ~~	ἀπόστολοις
κύριου	οἴκος	οὐρανοί
δούλον	γινώσκομεν	ἀγγέλῳ
θάνατε	λάμβανω	οἴκον
δίδασκει	κύριοι	ἔχουσι

☐ Flashcards - (Add the new cards.)

Greek Workbook - Level 4
Copyright © 1995 by Karen Mohs

85

LET'S PRACTICE

Circle the correctly accented words under each rule.

1. The acute accent can stand only on one of the last three syllables.
   a. The acute stands on the antepenult.

ἀπόστολος	ἀποστόλος	ἀποστολός
βλεπουσί	βλέπουσι	βλεπούσι

   b. The acute stands on the penult.

διδασκείς	δίδασκεις	διδάσκεις
θάνατῳ	θανάτῳ	θανατῷ

   c. The acute stands on the ultima.

οὐράνον	οὔρανον	οὐρανόν
ἀδελφός	ἀδέλφος	ἄδελφος

2. The acute accent can stand on long or short syllables.
   a. The acute stands on a short syllable.

γινωσκώ	φέρετε	δωροίς
δούλε	ἄγγελος	λαμβανείς

   b. The acute stands on a long syllable.

δώρῳ	λογόν	καί
βλεπουσί	υἱέ	γινώσκετε

3. When the ultima is long, the acute accent cannot stand on the antepenult.

ἄνθρωπου	θανάτου	λάμβανεις
λαμβάνεις	ἄδελφου	θάνατου

4. When the ultima is short, the acute accent cannot stand on a long penult.

δώρα	λόγος	δούλοι
δούλε	δούλον	θάνατοι

☐ Flashcards

Lesson 18

GENERAL RULES OF ACCENT
The Circumflex Accent

1. The circumflex accent (ˆ) can stand only on one of the last two syllables.

   Examples:　δοῦλος　(The circumflex stands on the penult.)
   υἱῶν　(The circumflex stands on the ultima.)

2. The circumflex accent (ˆ) can stand only on long syllables.

   Incorrect:　λῦγον
   Correct:　δῶρον

3. When the ultima is long, the circumflex accent (ˆ) cannot stand on the penult.

   Incorrect:　ἀνθρῶποις
   Correct:　ἀνθρώποις

4. When the ultima is short and the penult is long and is accented, the accent must be a circumflex (ˆ).

   Incorrect:　δούλος
   Correct:　δοῦλος

Write the words at the right under the correct headings.

Can be accented this way	**Cannot** be accented this way

δούλῳ
δῶρα
γινώσκουσι
δοῦλε
οἴκου
υἱῶν
οἴκον
θεὸς

☐　Flashcards - (Add the new cards.)

Greek Workbook - Level 4
Copyright © 1995 by Karen Mohs

87

LET'S PRACTICE

Circle the correctly accented words under each rule.

1. The circumflex accent can stand only on one of the last two syllables.

   a. The circumflex stands on the penult.

νομός	οἶκον	ἀγγελοῖ
δοῦλος	ἱερᾶ	κῦριον
δωρά	δῶρα	δῶρα

   b. The circumflex stands on the ultima.

ἀδελφῷ	ᾆδελφω	ἀδῆλφω
υἱοίς	υἱοῖς	υἷοις
οὐρανῶν	οὐρᾶνων	οὖρανων

2. The circumflex accent can stand only on long syllables.

υῖιου	υιῶς	υἱοῦ
θεῦς	θεοῖς	θῆεοις
δοῦλον	δουλῶν	θεῆ

3. When the ultima is long, the circumflex accent cannot stand on the penult.

δοῦλῳ	ᾆγεις	δούλῳ
κῦσμῳ	οἴκων	οἶκων
δῶροις	τῆκνων	δῶροις

4. When the ultima is short and the penult is long and is accented, the accent must be a circumflex.

δῶρον	δώρον	δωρῶν
δουλῆ	δούλε	δοῦλε
οἰκῦς	οἶκος	οἷκος

   [ ] Flashcards

LET'S PRACTICE

Write the words in the correct columns.

μένουσι	λύει	γράφομεν	θεῷ
οὐρανέ	ἀδελφέ	βάλλει	ἄνθρωπον
ἱεροῦ	οἶκος	δοῦλοι	τόπον
υἱοί	δῶρα	οὐρανοῖς	ἄγγελον
οἶκον	θεούς	λίθων	υἱῶν

acute accent on antepenult
_____
_____
_____
_____

acute accent on penult
_____
_____
_____
_____

acute accent on ultima
_____
_____
_____
_____

circumflex accent on penult
_____
_____
_____
_____

circumflex accent on ultima
_____
_____
_____
_____

☐ Flashcards

LET'S PRACTICE

Circle the word in each box that is accented correctly.

ἀποστόλον ἀποστολῶν ἀπόστολον	λίθῳ λῖθῳ λιθῶ	δωρᾶ δῶρα δώρα
γρᾶφει γράφει γραφεῖ	οὐρανῷ οὗρανῳ οὐρᾶνῳ	ἀδελφῶν ἀδελῶν ἀδελφῶν
ἀδελφου ἀδελφου ἀδελφοῦ	λεῖγει λέγει λεῖγει	μένομεν μένομεν μενομεν
θάνατον θανατῶν θανᾶτον	δουλῶς δούλος δοῦλος	λῶγοις λόγοις λογοῖς
υἵον υἱόν υἷον	ἀνθρώποι ἆνθρωποι ἄνθρωποι	θεούς θεῦς θεοῦς
βλεπῶμεν βλεπομεῖν βλέπομεν	λαμβάνουσι λάμβανουσι λαμβᾶνουσι	ἱερα ἱερά ἱερα

☐ Flashcards

90

Greek Workbook - Level 4
Copyright © 1995 by Karen Mohs

Lesson 19

GENERAL RULES OF ACCENT
The Grave Accent

1. The grave accent (`` ` ``) can stand only on the last syllable.
   Incorrect: ἀδὲλφος or ἀ̂δελφος
   Correct: ἀδελφὸς

2. When a word has an acute accent on its last syllable and it is followed immediately (without punctuation) by another word, the acute accent is changed to a grave accent (`` ` ``).
   Correct: υἱός
   Incorrect: υἱός ἀνθρώπου
   Correct: υἱὸς ἀνθρώπου

Accent the underlined words. Write what the sentences mean.

1. γινώσκομεν τὸν <u>ἀδελφον</u> τοῦ ἀποστόλου.

   It means _____

2. βλέπετε τὸν κύριον καὶ τὸν <u>ἀδελφον</u>.

   It means _____

3. ὁ <u>ἀδελφος</u> φέρει τοὺς λίθους καὶ γινώσκει τὸν οἶκον.

   It means _____

4. ἀκούω τὸν <u>ἀδελφον</u> καὶ γράφω τοὺς λόγους.

   It means _____

5. ὁ <u>ἀδελφος</u> τοῦ τέκνου μένει.

   It means _____

6. <u>ἀδελφοι</u>, βλέπω τὸν τόπον τοῦ ἱεροῦ.

   It means _____

☐ Flashcards - (Add the new cards.)

Greek Workbook - Level 4
Copyright © 1995 by Karen Mohs

91

LET'S PRACTICE

Circle the correctly accented words. Write what the sentences mean.

1. (μένω, μὲνω) τῷ υἱῷ τοῦ θεοῦ.

   It means _____

2. κύριε, τὸ τέκνον τοῦ (κὸσμου, κόσμου) λύει τὸ δῶρον.

   It means _____

3. οἱ ἀδελφοὶ ἄγουσι τοὺς δούλους τοῦ (οἴκου, οἶκου).

   It means _____

4. οἱ (ἄγγελοι, ἇγγελοι) ἀκούουσι τοὺς λόγους τοῦ κυρίου.

   It means _____

5. ὁ ἄνθρωπος φέρει τὸν (λῖθον, λίθον).

   It means _____

6. (πέμπω, πὲμπω) τὰ δῶρα καὶ διδάσκω τὸ τέκνον τῶν δούλων.

   It means _____

7. βλέπεις τὸν οὐρανόν, καὶ βλέπει τὸν (θάνατον, θᾶνατον).

   It means _____

8. ὁ λόγος τοῦ νόμου (δίδασκει, διδάσκει) τοὺς υἱοὺς ἀνθρώπων.

   It means _____

9. γινώσκω τὸν (οἴκον, οἶκον) καὶ βάλλω τοὺς λίθους.

   It means _____

10. ὁ κύριος ἐγείρει τὸ τέκνον τοῦ (δούλου, δοῦλου).

    It means _____

☐ Flashcards

92

Greek Workbook - Level 4
Copyright © 1995 by Karen Mohs

Lesson 20

RULE OF VERB ACCENT

The accent on a verb wants to be as close to the front of the word as it can.

1. If the ultima is short, put the accent on the antepenult. (If there is no antepenult, put it on the penult.)

2. If the ultima is long, put the accent on the penult.

Follow the accent rules we have learned to know which accent to use.

On the following verbs, underline the syllables that need accents. Accent the the underlined syllables.

λεγομεν	βαλλουσι	ἐχουσι
λυουσι	γραφομεν	ἀκουει
λαμβανεις	φερω	διδασκεις
διδασκει	ἐχετε	βλεπομεν
μενομεν	γινωσκεις	βαλλει
φερετε	ἀκουεις	λυω
γραφει	λεγεις	ἐγειρετε
ἐχεις	βλεπετε	γινωσκουσι
ἀκουομεν	λαμβανομεν	ἀγει
ἀγω	διδασκω	γραφω
γινωσκετε	φερουσι	λαμβανετε
βλεπουσι	ἐγειρω	λεγω

Remember!

SHORT VOWELS
α   a in *father*
ε   e in *get*
ο   o in *obey*
ι   i in *pit*
υ   oo in *good*

LONG VOWELS
α   a in *father*, held longer
η   a in *late*
ω   o in *note*
ι   ee in *feet*
υ   oo in *good*, held longer

DIPHTHONGS
αι   οι   ου
ει   αυ   υι
      ευ

☐ Flashcards - (Add the new cards.)

Greek Workbook - Level 4
Copyright © 1995 by Karen Mohs

93

LET'S PRACTICE

Write the Greek verbs with the correct accents.

we have _____

he remains _____

he raises up _____

they say _____

you (plural) lead _____

he takes _____

he destroys _____

he bears _____

you (singular) know _____

we write _____

we put _____

I teach _____

they remain _____

I send _____

you (plural) hear _____

I bring _____

☐ Flashcards

94

Greek Workbook - Level 4
Copyright © 1995 by Karen Mohs

Lesson 21

RULE OF NOUN ACCENT

The accent on a noun wants to stay where it is. Sometimes it has to move because of the accent rules we have learned.

1. In certain words, the accent stays where it started.

Example:

λόγος	λόγοι
λόγου	λόγων
λόγῳ	λόγοις
λόγον	λόγους
λόγε	λόγοι

2. In certain words, it stays where it started, but it changes form.

Example:

δοῦλος	δοῦλοι
δούλου	δούλων
δούλῳ	δούλοις
δοῦλον	δούλους
δοῦλε	δοῦλοι

3. In certain words, it must move to another syllable, but it always wants to get back to where it started.

Example:

ἄγγελος	ἄγγελοι
ἀγγέλου	ἀγγέλων
ἀγγέλῳ	ἀγγέλοις
ἄγγελον	ἀγγέλους
ἄγγελε	ἄγγελοι

Nouns with an acute accent on the ultima [like υἱός] have a special rule. The accent changes to a circumflex in the genitive and dative cases, both in singular and in plural.

Fill in the statements with the word **nouns** or the word **verbs**.

1. In _____, the accent wants to stay where it starts.

2. In _____, the accent wants to move to the front of the word.

☐ Flashcards - (Add the new card.)

Greek Workbook - Level 4
Copyright © 1995 by Karen Mohs

95

LET'S PRACTICE

On the following nouns, underline the syllable that needs the accent. Put an acute or a circumflex accent on the underlined syllable. (The first word in each row shows where the accent starts.)

(τέκνον)	τεκνων	τεκνῳ	τεκνοις
(κύριος)	κυριῳ	κυριοις	κυριοι
(τόπος)	τοποις	τοπου	τοπων
(υἱός)	υἱου	υἱοις	υἱε
(λίθος)	λιθοι	λιθου	λιθοις
(ἀπόστολος)	ἀποστολους	ἀποστολοι	ἀποστολων
(θάνατος)	θανατοις	θανατε	θανατου
(οἶκος)	οἰκους	οἰκοις	οἰκων
(θεός)	θεε	θεον	θεοι
(νόμος)	νομους	νομῳ	νομον
(λόγος)	λογων	λογοι	λογου
(οὐρανός)	οὐρανους	οὐρανου	οὐρανοι
(δῶρον)	δωρα	δωρῳ	δωροις
(ἄγγελος)	ἀγγελου	ἀγγελοις	ἀγγελων
(δοῦλος)	δουλῳ	δουλον	δουλοι
(κόσμος)	κοσμου	κοσμῳ	κοσμον
(ἱερόν)	ἱερῳ	ἱερα	ἱερου

☐ Flashcards

96

Greek Workbook - Level 4
Copyright © 1995 by Karen Mohs

LET'S PRACTICE

Accent the following Greek nouns. Write what they mean.

τεκνον _____	τεκνα _____
τεκνου _____	τεκνων _____
τεκνῳ _____	τεκνοις _____
τεκνον _____	τεκνα _____
τεκνον _____	τεκνα _____

λιθος _____	λιθοι _____
λιθου _____	λιθων _____
λιθῳ _____	λιθοις _____
λιθον _____	λιθους _____
λιθε _____	λιθοι _____

υιος _____	υιοι _____
υιου _____	υιων _____
υιῳ _____	υιοις _____
υιον _____	υιους _____
υιε _____	υιοι _____

☐ Flashcards

Greek Workbook - Level 4
Copyright © 1995 by Karen Mohs

97

LET'S PRACTICE

Accent the underlined words. Write what the sentences mean.

1. πέμπω τὰ <u>δωρα</u> καὶ τὸν λίθον.

   It means _____

2. ὁ <u>ἀγγελος</u> θανάτου γράφει τὸν νόμον τοῦ κόσμου.

   It means _____

3. οἱ δοῦλοι τοῦ τέκνου βάλλουσι τοὺς <u>λιθους</u>.

   It means _____

4. οἱ υἱοὶ τοῦ <u>θεου</u> βλέπουσιν οὐρανὸν καὶ τὸν κόσμον.

   It means _____

5. ὁ κύριος ἄγει ἀνθρώπους καὶ <u>ἐγειρει</u> τὸ τέκνον.

   It means _____

6. μένω καὶ ἀκούω <u>τους</u> λόγους τοῦ θεοῦ.

   It means _____

7. υἱοί, βλέπετε τὸν κύριον καὶ γινώσκετε τὸν <u>θεον</u>.

   It means _____

8. ὁ <u>νομος</u> τοῦ θεοῦ διδάσκει τὸν ἄνθρωπον.

   It means _____

9. φέρω τοὺς νόμους καὶ βλέπω τοὺς οἴκους τῶν <u>ἀποστολων</u>.

   It means _____

10. οἱ <u>ἀδελφοι</u> τοῦ κόσμου γινώσκουσι τοὺς ἀποστόλους τοῦ κυρίου.

    It means _____

☐ Flashcards

98

Greek Workbook - Level 4
Copyright © 1995 by Karen Mohs

Lesson 22

WORD ORDER

The usual word order in a Greek sentence is like an English sentence.

SUBJECT - VERB - DIRECT OBJECT

However, if you want to call attention to a certain word or phrase,
put it at the beginning of the sentence.

The word order can also be changed to make the sentence sound better.

Write the sentences in Greek, giving three different word orders for each one.

1. Men throw stones.

   a. _____

   b. _____

   c. _____

2. An apostle leads a brother.

   a. _____

   b. _____

   c. _____

3. A servant brings a son.

   a. _____

   b. _____

   c. _____

□ Flashcards

Greek Workbook - Level 4
Copyright © 1995 by Karen Mohs

PUNCTUATION

Greek has four punctuation marks.

1. The comma (,)
   It is used like our English comma.

2. The period (.)
   It is used like our English period.

3. The colon (·)
   This looks like only the top half of our English colon.
   It is used like our English colon and our English semicolon.

4. The question mark (;)
   This looks like our English semicolon, but it is really a
   Greek question mark.

Beside each English punctuation mark, write the Greek one.

English	Greek		English	Greek		English	Greek		English	Greek		English	Greek
,	____		.	____		:	____		;	____		?	____

Fill in the blanks with the correct punctuation marks.

1. To end a Greek sentence that asks a question, we use a _____.

2. To end a Greek sentence that makes a statement, we use a _____.

3. In English we use a semicolon, in Greek we use a _____.

4. In English we use a comma, in Greek we use a _____.

5. In English we use a colon, in Greek we use a _____.

☐ Flashcards - (Add the new cards.)

100

Greek Workbook - Level 4
Copyright © 1995 by Karen Mohs

Lesson 23

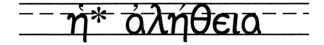

means

the truth

It sounds like hay a-**lay**-thay-ah.

Write the Greek word that means **the truth**.

Circle the correct words.

the place	I remain	the heaven
ὁ κόσμος	ἔχω	ὁ οὐρανός
ὁ υἱός	μένω	ὁ οἶκος
ὁ τόπος	λέγω	ὁ θάνατος
I bring	the child	I put
ἐγείρω	τὸ τέκνον	ἄγω
φέρω	ὁ ἄγγελος	λύω
λαμβάνω	τὸ ἱερόν	βάλλω
the truth	I send	the stone
ἡ ἀλήθεια	βλέπω	ὁ κύριος
ὁ θεός	γινώσκω	ὁ λίθος
ὁ νόμος	πέμπω	τὸ δῶρον

*All the nouns learned so far have been masculine (ὁ) or neuter (τό). Now we begin to learn the feminine nouns. Feminine nouns have the article ἡ.

☐ Flashcards - (Add the new card.)

LET'S PRACTICE

Write the Greek word that means **the truth**.

Write the Greek words.

the child

the truth

the son

the heaven

the place

☐ Flashcards

means

the kingdom

It sounds like hay ba-si-**lay**-ah.

Write the Greek word that means **the kingdom**.

_____

Match the Greek words to their meanings.

____	1. ὁ λίθος	a.	the child
____	2. τὸ τέκνον	b.	the stone
____	3. ἡ ἀλήθεια	c.	the place
____	4. ὁ τόπος	d.	the heaven
____	5. ὁ οὐρανός	e.	the kingdom
____	6. ἡ βασιλεία	f.	the death
____	7. ὁ θάνατος	g.	the truth
____	8. πέμπω	h.	I bear
____	9. ἄγω	i.	I send
____	10. φέρω	j.	I lead
____	11. ἔχω	k.	I have
____	12. μένω	l.	I raise up
____	13. ἐγείρω	m.	I cast
____	14. βάλλω	n.	I remain

☐ Flashcards - (Add the new card.)

LET'S PRACTICE

Write the Greek word that means **the kingdom**.

Write the Greek words.

the truth

the angel

the kingdom

the place

the word

☐ Flashcards

means

the day

It sounds like hay hay-**me**-rah.

Write the Greek word that means **the day**.

Circle the words that mean the same as the first words in the rows.

I send	πέμπω	ἐγείρω	γράφω
the kingdom	ὁ νόμος	ἡ βασιλεία	ὁ ἀπόστολος
I remain	ἄγω	λέγω	μένω
the heaven	τὸ ἱερόν	ὁ οἶκος	ὁ οὐρανός
the day	ἡ ἡμέρα	ὁ δοῦλος	ἡ ἀλήθεια
the child	ὁ υἱός	ὁ ἀδελφός	τὸ τέκνον
I throw	βάλλω	λύω	διδάσκω
I bring	βλέπω	φέρω	γινώσκω
the world	ὁ κόσμος	ὁ λόγος	ὁ ἄνθρωπος
the truth	τὸ δῶρον	ὁ ἄγγελος	ἡ ἀλήθεια
the stone	ὁ λίθος	ὁ θάνατος	τὸ ἱερόν
the place	ὁ θεός	ὁ τόπος	ὁ κύριος

☐ Flashcards - (Add the new card.)

LET'S PRACTICE

Write the Greek word that means **the day**.

Write the Greek words.

the place

the truth

the kingdom

the servant

the day

☐ Flashcards

Lesson 24

ἡ καρδία

means

the heart

It sounds like hay kar-**dee**-ah.

Write the Greek word that means **the heart**.

_____

Write the meanings of the following Greek words.

πέμπω _____

ὁ τόπος _____

ἡ ἡμέρα _____

ὁ οὐρανός _____

ἡ βασιλεία _____

ἄγω _____

ἡ καρδία _____

ἐγείρω _____

μένω _____

ὁ κόσμος _____

ἡ ἀλήθεια _____

ὁ λίθος _____

ὁ θάνατος _____

τὸ τέκνον _____

βάλλω _____

☐ Flashcards - (Add the new card.)

Greek Workbook - Level 4
Copyright © 1995 by Karen Mohs

LET'S PRACTICE

Write the Greek word that means **the heart**.

Write the Greek words.

the day

the truth

the heart

the apostle

the kingdom

☐ Flashcards

108

Greek Workbook - Level 4
Copyright © 1995 by Karen Mohs

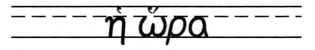

means

the hour

It sounds like hay **ho**-rah.

Write the Greek word that means **the hour**.

_____

Match the words to their meanings.

ἡ καρδία	the heart
πέμπω	the hour
ἡ ὥρα	I bear
ὁ λίθος	I send
φέρω	the stone
ὁ οὐρανός	the truth
ἡ ἀλήθεια	the Lord
ἡ βασιλεία	the heaven
ὁ κύριος	the kingdom
ὁ τόπος	the child
μένω	the place
ἡ ἡμέρα	I remain
τὸ τέκνον	the day
βάλλω	I put

☐ Flashcards - (Add the new card.)

LET'S PRACTICE

Write the Greek word that means **the hour**.

Write the Greek words.

the law

the brother

the heart

the day

the hour

☐ Flashcards

ἡ ἐκκλησία

means

the church

It sounds like hay ek-klay-**see**-ah.

Write the Greek word that means **the church**.

Circle the correct words.

the hour	I send	the kingdom
ἡ ἀλήθεια	ἐγείρω	ἡ βασιλεία
ἡ δόξα	πέμπω	ἡ ἀλήθεια
ἡ ὥρα	ἄγω	ἡ καρδία
the word	**the day**	**I bear**
ὁ νόμος	ἡ ἡμέρα	μένω
ὁ λόγος	ἡ ὥρα	βάλλω
ὁ οἶκος	ἡ δόξα	φέρω
the heart	**the church**	**the truth**
ἡ καρδία	ἡ βασιλεία	ἡ ἐκκλησία
ἡ ἐκκλησία	ἡ καρδία	ἡ ἀλήθεια
ἡ ὥρα	ἡ ἐκκλησία	ἡ ἡμέρα

☐ Flashcards - (Add the new card.)

Greek Workbook - Level 4
Copyright © 1995 by Karen Mohs

LET'S PRACTICE

Write the Greek word that means **the church**.

Write the Greek words.

the place

the church

the hour

the man

the heart

☐ Flashcards

112

LET'S PRACTICE

Write the Greek words.

the world _____

the kingdom _____

the heaven _____

the child _____

the hour _____

the church _____

the gift _____

the truth _____

the stone _____

the heart _____

the temple _____

the place _____

the house _____

the day _____

the angel _____

the law _____

☐ Flashcards

Greek Workbook - Level 4
Copyright © 1995 by Karen Mohs

113

PUZZLE TIME

Find eighteen Greek words in the puzzle below. (Accents and breathing marks have been left off.)

β	ε	ζ	η	φ	κ	δ	ν	ε	γ	ε	ι	ρ	ω	λ	ε	π	θ	ι	δ	ζ	s
α	λ	η	θ	ε	ι	α	ρ	η	τ	α	ο	φ	γ	κ	υ	κ	υ	ρ	ι	ο	s
σ	π	μ	κ	ο	σ	τ	ρ	ω	ξ	χ	θ	α	ν	α	τ	ο	s	χ	δ	ξ	η
ι	λ	ε	ψ	λ	μ	γ	χ	δ	δ	ω	ε	μ	ψ	κ	ψ	σ	β	κ	α	ι	υ
λ	τ	ρ	η	ε	ι	α	ε	λ	ι	ρ	ο	σ	β	ο	ν	μ	θ	φ	σ	ο	μ
ε	ν	α	ω	γ	s	θ	φ	ω	ρ	α	s	ε	ω	υ	ξ	ο	ρ	μ	κ	π	ε
ι	δ	ξ	β	ω	ι	ν	ο	ψ	α	θ	υ	λ	υ	ω	χ	s	ι	λ	ω	τ	ν
α	γ	ω	μ	υ	γ	ρ	κ	s	π	β	ζ	ι	ο	δ	κ	σ	ζ	α	γ	θ	ω

Write the words you found. Remember to add the breathing marks and accents.

1. _____   10. _____

2. _____   11. _____

3. _____   12. _____

4. _____   13. _____

5. _____   14. _____

6. _____   15. _____

7. _____   16. _____

8. _____   17. _____

9. _____   18. _____

☐ Flashcards

114

Greek Workbook - Level 4
Copyright © 1995 by Karen Mohs

Lesson 25

FEMININE NOUNS

Nouns that have the article ἡ are feminine.
These nouns usually end in α or η.

Write the nouns in the box under the correct definite articles.

δῶρον	ἀλήθεια	θεός
λίθος	κόσμος	ἡμέρα
θάνατος	ὥρα	τέκνον
βασιλεία	ἱερόν	καρδία
κύριος	οὐρανός	τόπος
	ἐκκλησία	

ὁ   τό   ἡ

☐ Flashcards

Greek Workbook - Level 4
Copyright © 1995 by Karen Mohs

115

LET'S PRACTICE

Circle the genders for these Greek nouns.

ἀπόστολος	masculine	feminine	neuter
ὥρα	masculine	feminine	neuter
ἀδελφός	masculine	feminine	neuter
νόμος	masculine	feminine	neuter
δοῦλος	masculine	feminine	neuter
τέκνον	masculine	feminine	neuter
υἱός	masculine	feminine	neuter
ἀλήθεια	masculine	feminine	neuter
ἄγγελος	masculine	feminine	neuter
δῶρον	masculine	feminine	neuter
κύριος	masculine	feminine	neuter
καρδία	masculine	feminine	neuter
οἶκος	masculine	feminine	neuter
ἱερόν	masculine	feminine	neuter
λόγος	masculine	feminine	neuter
ἡμέρα	masculine	feminine	neuter
ἐκκλησία	masculine	feminine	neuter
βασιλεία	masculine	feminine	neuter

☐ Flashcards

MORE ON FEMININE NOUNS

In feminine nouns that have an ε, ι, or ρ before the final α,
that final α is long.

Singular

Nominative	ἡ καρδία	means	**the heart.** (*subject of sentence*)
Genitive	τῆς καρδίας	means	**of the heart.** (*shows possession*)
Dative	τῇ καρδίᾳ	means	**to (or for) the heart.** (*indirect object*)
Accusative	τὴν καρδίαν	means	**the heart.** (*direct object*)
Vocative	καρδία	means	**heart.** (*direct address*)

Match the words to their meanings.

ἡ ἀλήθεια*	the day
τῇ ὥρᾳ	the truth
τὴν ἡμέραν	to the hour
τὴν βασιλείαν	for the church
ἡ καρδία	the heart
τῇ ἐκκλησίᾳ	the kingdom
τῇ βασιλείᾳ	for the kingdom
τὴν καρδίαν	the heart
τῆς ἡμέρας	of the day
τὴν ἐκκλησίαν	the truth
τῇ ἡμέρᾳ	the church
τὴν ἀλήθειαν	to the day
ἡ ὥρα	of the truth
τῇ καρδίᾳ	for the heart
τῆς ἀληθείας	the hour

*In ἀλήθεια and ἀλήθειαν, the last α is short instead of long. This exception occurs in only a few words.

☐ Flashcards - (Add the new cards.)

Greek Workbook - Level 4
Copyright © 1995 by Karen Mohs

117

LET'S PRACTICE

Finish the words with the correct endings.

1. ἡ ὡρ_____ means **the hour**.

2. τῇ καρδί_____ means **for the heart**.

3. τὴν ἀλήθει_____ means **the truth**.

4. τῆς ἡμέρ_____ means **of the day**.

5. τὴν ὡρ_____ means **the hour**.

6. ἡ καρδί_____ means **the heart**.

7. τῆς ἀληθεί_____ means **of the truth**.

8. τὴν καρδί_____ means **the heart**.

9. τὴν ἡμέρ_____ means **the day**.

10. τῇ βασιλεί_____ means **for the kingdom**.

11. τῆς καρδί_____ means **of the heart**.

12. ἡ βασιλεί_____ means **the kingdom**.

13. τῆς ὡρ_____ means **of the hour**.

14. τὴν βασιλεί_____ means **the kingdom**.

15. τῇ ἡμέρ_____ means **to the day**.

☐ Flashcards

118

LET'S PRACTICE

Choose the best words for the sentences below. Put them in the blanks.
Write what the sentences mean.

τόπῳ	βλέπεις	ἀληθείας

1. ὁ θεὸς τῆς _____ γινώσκει τὴν καρδίαν ἀνθρώπου.

   It means _____

2. ἀδελφέ, _____ τὰ ἱερὰ τῆς βασιλείας.

   It means _____

3. οἱ ἄγγελοι λέγουσι τὴν ἀλήθειαν τῷ _____.

   It means _____

πέμπω	τέκνον	οὐρανόν

1. _____ καὶ ἀπόστολος γινώσκουσι τὴν ὥραν.

   It means _____

2. ἡ ἡμέρα τοῦ κυρίου φέρει _____.

   It means _____

3. _____ τὰ δῶρα καὶ γινώσκω τὸ τέκνον.

   It means _____

☐ Flashcards

Greek Workbook - Level 4
Copyright © 1995 by Karen Mohs

119

LET'S PRACTICE

Read these Greek sentences. Write what they mean.

1. ἡ καρδία τοῦ τέκνου γινώσκει τὴν ἀλήθειαν τοῦ κυρίου.

   It means _____

2. γράφομεν τοὺς λόγους τῆς βασιλείας τῷ κόσμῳ.

   It means _____

3. διδάσκεις τὸ τέκνον· τὸ τέκνον διδάσκει τοὺς υἱούς.

   It means _____

4. οἱ λόγοι τοῦ κυρίου ἄγουσι τὸν κόσμον.

   It means _____

5. λαμβάνω τοὺς ἀποστόλους καὶ γινώσκω τοὺς τόπους ἀνθρώπων.

   It means _____

6. ὁ θεὸς ἐγείρει τὸν ἄνθρωπον· ὁ ἄνθρωπος γινώσκει τὴν ὥραν.

   It means _____

7. λαμβάνετε τὸ δῶρον οὐρανοῦ· λύετε τοὺς δούλους θανάτου.

   It means _____

8. οἱ ἀδελφοὶ βάλλουσι τοὺς λίθους, καὶ πέμπω τοὺς ἀγγέλους.

   It means _____

9. φέρετε τοὺς λίθους τοῦ οἴκου· φέρω τοὺς λίθους τοῦ ἱεροῦ.

   It means _____

10. ἔχομεν τὴν ἀλήθειαν τῶν λόγων τῶν ἀποστόλων.

    It means _____

☐ Flashcards

Lesson 26

means

the glory

It sounds like hay **do**-xah.

Write the Greek word that means **the glory**.

Circle the correct words.

the day	ὁ οὐρανός ὁ θεός ἡ ἡμέρα	the truth	ὁ λόγος τὸ τέκνον ἡ ἀλήθεια
the stone	ὁ κύριος ὁ λίθος ὁ δοῦλος	the glory	ἡ δόξα ὁ οἶκος ὁ θάνατος
the kingdom	τὸ ἱερόν ὁ νόμος ἡ βασιλεία	the hour	τὸ δῶρον ἡ ὥρα ὁ ἀπόστολος
the heart	ἡ καρδία ὁ ἀδελφός ὁ υἱός	the world	ὁ ἄγγελος ὁ τόπος ὁ κόσμος

☐ Flashcards - (Add the new card.)

LET'S PRACTICE

Write the Greek word that means **the glory**.

Write the Greek words.

the hour

the kingdom

the day

the glory

the heart

☐ Flashcards

LET'S PRACTICE

Write the Greek words.

the church _____

I raise up _____

I throw _____

the heart _____

I hear _____

I loose _____

the glory _____

I remain _____

the truth _____

I say _____

I lead _____

I have _____

the kingdom _____

I take _____

I bring _____

the day _____

☐ Flashcards

PUZZLE TIME

Think of the meanings of the English words. Write the Greek words on the puzzle below. (Do not include the accents or the breathing marks.)

across

2. I see
8. a glory
10. a lord
11. I remain
12. a day
13. a death
15. I take
18. a temple
19. a world
20. a place
21. I raise up
23. I have
24. a kingdom
27. I lead
28. a house
31. a heaven
32. I say
33. God
34. a word
35. a servant

down

1. I bring
3. I send
4. I destroy
5. I know
6. a brother
7. I teach
8. a gift
9. a truth
10. a heart
14. an angel
16. I hear
17. an apostle
20. a child
22. I write
25. a stone
26. a law
29. an hour
30. I cast

☐ Flashcards

124

Greek Workbook - Level 4
Copyright © 1995 by Karen Mohs

Lesson 27

MORE ON FEMININE NOUNS

In feminine nouns that have σ, λλ, ζ, ξ, or ψ before the final α,
that final α is short.

Singular

Nominative	ἡ δόξα	means	**the glory.** (*subject of sentence*)
Genitive	τῆς δόξης	means	**of the glory.** (*shows possession*)
Dative	τῇ δόξῃ	means	**to (or for) the glory.** (*indirect object*)
Accusative	τὴν δόξαν	means	**the glory.** (*direct object*)
Vocative	δόξα	means	**glory.** (*direct address*)

Circle the correct words.

of the truth	to the kingdom	the day
τὴν ἀλήθειαν τῆς ἀληθείας τῇ ἀληθείᾳ	τῇ βασιλείᾳ ἡ βασιλεία τῆς βασιλείας	τῆς ἡμέρας τῇ ἡμέρᾳ ἡ ἡμέρα
the hour	**the truth**	**of the heart**
τὴν ὥραν τῇ ὥρᾳ τῆς ὥρας	τῇ ἀληθείᾳ ἡ ἀλήθεια τῆς ἀληθείας	τῆς καρδίας τὴν καρδίαν τῇ καρδίᾳ
the kingdom	**of the church**	**for the glory**
τῆς βασιλείας τῇ βασιλείᾳ τὴν βασιλείαν	ἡ ἐκκλησία τῆς ἐκκλησίας τῇ ἐκκλησίᾳ	τῇ δόξῃ ἡ δόξα τῆς δόξης
for the day	**the heart**	**the church**
τῇ ἡμέρᾳ τῆς ἡμέρας τὴν ἡμέραν	τῇ καρδίᾳ τῆς καρδίας ἡ καρδία	τῇ ἐκκλησίᾳ τὴν ἐκκλησίαν τῆς ἐκκλησίας

☐ Flashcards - (Add the new cards.)

Greek Workbook - Level 4
Copyright © 1995 by Karen Mohs

LET'S PRACTICE

Circle the correct articles. Write what the sentences mean.

1. γράφω (ὁ, τὴν) ἀλήθειαν (τῆς, τῇ) δόξης τοῦ θεοῦ.

    It means _____

2. (τὴν, ἡ) ἡμέρα (τῆς, ἡ) ἐκκλησίας λύει τὰ ἱερὰ τῶν ἀνθρώπων.

    It means _____

3. πέμπω (τὰ, τὸν) δῶρα (τοῦ, τοῖς) τέκνου τῶν δούλων.

    It means _____

4. λαμβάνομεν (τὸν, τοὺς) λίθους· βλέπομεν (τοὺς, τοῖς) οἴκους.

    It means _____

5. (οἱ, ὁ) κόσμος ἄγει τοὺς ἀδελφούς, καὶ διδάσκεις (τὰ, τὸν) νόμον.

    It means _____

6. (ἡ, ὁ) ἀλήθεια τοῦ λόγου φέρει (τὴν, τῆς) δόξαν.

    It means _____

7. (τῇ, ἡ) ἐκκλησία ἀκούει τὴν ἀλήθειαν, καὶ βλέπεις τὴν βασιλείαν.

    It means _____

8. ἀκούεις τὸν ἄγγελον (τῆς, τὴν) ἀληθείας καὶ γινώσκεις τὴν ὥραν.

    It means _____

9. βλέπετε (τὴν, τῇ) ἐκκλησίαν καὶ (τὸ, τοῦ) ἱερὸν τοῦ κυρίου.

    It means _____

10. (ἡ, τῆς) ὥρα διδάσκει τοὺς ἀνθρώπους· ἔχουσι (ἡ, τὴν) ἀλήθειαν.

    It means _____

☐ Flashcards

126

Greek Workbook - Level 4
Copyright © 1995 by Karen Mohs

LET'S PRACTICE

Match the Greek sentences to their meanings.

_____ 1. ἔχει καρδίαν λίθου.　　　a. He has a house of stone.

_____ 2. ἔχει οἶκον λίθου.　　　b. He has a heart of stone.

_____ 3. υἱέ, γινώσκω.　　　c. Son, I know.

_____ 4. γινώσκω υἱόν.　　　d. I know a son.

_____ 5. ἄγει ἐκκλησίαν.　　　e. He leads a church.

_____ 6. ἐκκλησία ἄγει.　　　f. A church leads.

_____ 7. βασιλεία μένει.　　　g. Truth remains.

_____ 8. ἀλήθεια μένει.　　　h. A kingdom remains.

_____ 9. βάλλομεν λίθον.　　　i. We throw the stone.

_____ 10. βάλλομεν τὸν λίθον.　　　j. We throw a stone.

_____ 11. ἐγείρω τέκνον.　　　k. I raise up a child.

_____ 12. ἐγείρει τέκνον.　　　l. He raises up a child.

_____ 13. ἀκούω τὸν κύριον.　　　m. The Lord hears.

_____ 14. ὁ κύριος ἀκούει.　　　n. I hear the Lord.

_____ 15. λύουσι τὸν κόσμον.　　　o. They destroy the world.

_____ 16. λύετε τὸν κόσμον.　　　p. You destroy the world.

_____ 17. διδάσκω νόμον.　　　q. I teach a law.

_____ 18. νόμος διδάσκει.　　　r. A law teaches.

_____ 19. γράφομεν λόγον.　　　s. We write the word.

_____ 20. γράφομεν τὸν λόγον.　　　t. We write a word.

☐ Flashcards

Greek Workbook - Level 4
Copyright © 1995 by Karen Mohs

127

LET'S PRACTICE

Write the meanings of the Greek sentences on the lines beneath the sentences.

ὁ ἄνθρωπος τοῦ θεοῦ ἄγει· ὁ ἄνθρωπος θανάτου λύει.

_____

ἄνθρωποι τοῦ θεοῦ ἄγουσιν· ἄνθρωποι θανάτου λύουσιν.

_____

ὁ ἀπόστολος ἐγείρει τὴν δόξαν τῆς ἐκκλησίας τοῦ θεοῦ.

_____

ἀπόστολος ἐγείρει δόξαν τῇ ἐκκλησίᾳ τοῦ θεοῦ.

_____

διδάσκω τὸν λόγον τοῦ θεοῦ· γράφω τὸν νόμον ἀνθρώπων.

_____

διδάσκεις λόγον ἀνθρώπων· γράφομεν τοὺς νόμους ἀνθρώποις.

_____

ἀδελφοὶ γινώσκουσι τὴν ἡμέραν· ἀπόστολοι γινώσκουσι τὴν ὥραν.

_____

ἀδελφὸς γινώσκει ἡμέραν· ἀπόστολος γινώσκει ὥραν.

_____

ἡ καρδία τοῦ τέκνου φέρει δῶρα· ἀκούει τὴν ἀλήθειαν.

_____

ἡ καρδία τέκνου φέρει δῶρον· ἀκούει τὸν λόγον.

_____

☐ Flashcards

128

Greek Workbook - Level 4
Copyright © 1995 by Karen Mohs

Lesson 28

means

the writing, the Scripture

It sounds like hay gra-**fay**.

Write the Greek word that means **the writing** or **the Scripture**.
_____
- -
_____

Write the meanings of the following Greek words.

ἡ βασιλεία _____
ὁ οὐρανός _____
ἡ δόξα _____
ἡ γραφή _____
ὁ θάνατος _____
ἡ ἀλήθεια _____
ἡ καρδία _____
ὁ τόπος _____
ὁ λίθος _____
ὁ θεός _____
ἡ ἐκκλησία _____
ὁ κόσμος _____
ἡ ἡμέρα _____
τὸ τέκνον _____
ἡ ὥρα _____

☐ Flashcards - (Add the new card.)

LET'S PRACTICE

Write the Greek word that means **the writing** or **the Scripture**.

Write the Greek words.

the glory

the writing

the heart

the hour

the church

☐ Flashcards

means

the peace

It sounds like hay ay-**ray**-nay.

Write the Greek word that means **the peace**.

_____

Match the words to their meanings.

λύω	I lead
ἡ ὥρα	the truth
ἡ εἰρήνη	I loose
ἄγω	the hour
ἡ ἀλήθεια	the peace
ὁ οὐρανός	I hear
ἀκούω	the heaven
ἡ γραφή	I raise up
ἐγείρω	the Scripture
ὁ τόπος	the church
ἡ ἐκκλησία	the place
ὁ λίθος	the child
ἡ ἡμέρα	the stone
τὸ τέκνον	the day

☐ Flashcards - (Add the new card.)

LET'S PRACTICE

Write the Greek word that means **the peace**.

Write the Greek words.

the house

the world

the church

the Scripture

the peace

☐ Flashcards

132

Greek Workbook - Level 4
Copyright © 1995 by Karen Mohs

ἡ ἐντολή

means

the commandment

It sounds like hay en-to-**lay**.

Write the Greek word that means **the commandment**.

Match the Greek words to their meanings.

_____ 1. ἡ γραφή   a. the commandment

_____ 2. ἡ δόξα   b. the kingdom

_____ 3. ἡ βασιλεία   c. the writing

_____ 4. ἡ εἰρήνη   d. the glory

_____ 5. τὸ ἱερόν   e. the temple

_____ 6. ἡ ἐντολή   f. the heart

_____ 7. ἡ καρδία   g. the peace

_____ 8. φέρω   h. I raise up

_____ 9. βάλλω   i. I bear

_____ 10. ἐγείρω   j. I send

_____ 11. πέμπω   k. I cast

_____ 12. ἄγω   l. I destroy

_____ 13. λύω   m. I remain

_____ 14. μένω   n. I lead

☐ Flashcards - (Add the new card.)

Greek Workbook - Level 4
Copyright © 1995 by Karen Mohs

133

LET'S PRACTICE

Write the Greek word that means **the commandment**.

Write the Greek words.

the peace

the death

the Scripture

the son

the commandment

☐ Flashcards

134

Greek Workbook - Level 4
Copyright © 1995 by Karen Mohs

Lesson 29

means

the life

It sounds like hay dzo-**ay**.

Write the Greek word that means **the life**.

Circle the words that mean the same as the first words in the rows.

the church	ὁ κύριος	ὁ ἀδελφός	ἡ ἐκκλησία
I bring	φέρω	μένω	πέμπω
the truth	ὁ δοῦλος	ἡ ἀλήθεια	τὸ δῶρον
the place	ὁ τόπος	ὁ κόσμος	ἡ ἐντολή
the life	ὁ ἀπόστολος	ἡ ζωή	ὁ λόγος
the kingdom	ἡ βασιλεία	ὁ ἄνθρωπος	ὁ οὐρανός
the glory	τὸ τέκνον	ὁ ἄγγελος	ἡ δόξα
the writing	ἡ γραφή	ἡ ὥρα	ὁ οἶκος
the day	ὁ θεός	ἡ ἡμέρα	ὁ θάνατος
the peace	ἡ εἰρήνη	ὁ υἱός	ὁ νόμος
the heart	ὁ λίθος	ἡ καρδία	τὸ ἱερόν
I put	ἄγω	ἐγείρω	βάλλω

☐ Flashcards - (Add the new card.)

Greek Workbook - Level 4
Copyright © 1995 by Karen Mohs

LET'S PRACTICE

Write the Greek word that means **the life**.

Write the Greek words.

the commandment

the word

God

the life

the peace

☐ Flashcards

136

Greek Workbook - Level 4
Copyright © 1995 by Karen Mohs

ἡ παραβολή

means

the parable

It sounds like hay pa-ra-bo-**lay**.

Write the Greek word that means **the parable**.

Circle the correct words.

the heart	the peace	the Scripture
τὸ δῶρον	ὁ τόπος	ἡ γραφή
ἡ καρδία	ἡ εἰρήνη	ὁ θάνατος
ὁ κόσμος	ὁ ἄγγελος	ἡ βασιλεία
the glory	**the parable**	**the church**
ἡ δόξα	ὁ νόμος	ὁ οἶκος
ἡ ἡμέρα	ὁ οὐρανός	ἡ ἐκκλησία
ὁ θεός	ἡ παραβολή	ὁ λόγος
the life	**the hour**	**the commandment**
ἡ ζωή	ὁ υἱός	τὸ ἱερόν
ὁ κύριος	ἡ ὥρα	ἡ ἀλήθεια
τὸ τέκνον	ὁ λίθος	ἡ ἐντολή

☐ Flashcards - (Add the new card.)

Greek Workbook - Level 4
Copyright © 1995 by Karen Mohs

LET'S PRACTICE

Write the Greek word that means **the parable**.

Write the Greek words.

the Lord

the parable

the commandment

the life

the servant

☐ Flashcards

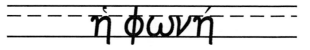

means

the voice

It sounds like hay fo-**nay**.

Write the Greek word that means **the voice**.

Circle the correct words.

the angel	ὁ ἄγγελος ἡ ἐντολή ὁ νόμος	the life	ἡ ἐκκλησία ὁ κύριος ἡ ζωή
the voice	ὁ κόσμος ἡ ἡμέρα ἡ φωνή	the hour	ἡ ὥρα ἡ βασιλεία ὁ τόπος
the writing	ἡ γραφή ὁ υἱός ὁ θάνατος	the parable	τὸ τέκνον ἡ παραβολή ὁ θεός
the peace	ὁ οὐρανός ἡ εἰρήνη ἡ ἀλήθεια	the glory	ὁ λίθος ἡ καρδία ἡ δόξα

☐ Flashcards - (Add the new card.)

LET'S PRACTICE

Write the Greek word that means **the voice**.

Write the Greek words.

the life

the parable

the apostle

the voice

the temple

☐ Flashcards

Lesson 30

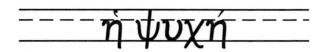

means

the soul

It sounds like hay psoo-**khay**.

Write the Greek word that means **the soul**.

_____

_____

Write the meanings of the following Greek words.

ἡ ἡμέρα _____

ἡ παραβολή _____

ἡ ἐκκλησία _____

μένω _____

ἡ καρδία _____

φέρω _____

ἡ ψυχή _____

ἡ ἐντολή _____

ἄγω _____

ἡ γραφή _____

ἡ φωνή _____

βάλλω _____

ἡ εἰρήνη _____

ἡ ζωή _____

ὁ τόπος _____

☐ Flashcards - (Add the new card.)

LET'S PRACTICE

Write the Greek word that means **the soul**.

Write the Greek words.

the gift

the soul

the voice

the life

the parable

☐ Flashcards

142

Greek Workbook - Level 4
Copyright © 1995 by Karen Mohs

LET'S PRACTICE

Write the Greek words.

the church _____

the heart _____

the life _____

the day _____

the soul _____

the parable _____

the stone _____

the Scripture _____

the kingdom _____

the glory _____

the peace _____

the child _____

the voice _____

the hour _____

the commandment _____

the truth _____

☐ Flashcards

PUZZLE TIME

Unscramble the Greek words.

ήηεἰνρ _____

οεἄλγσγ _____

ἡζω _____

ααίδρκ _____

οόsΤπ _____

ἑίαησκλκ _____

οοῖsκ _____

ειαἀήλθ _____

όεἰνρ _____

ἡωνφ _____

οόsμν _____

αόδξ _____

υήχψ _____

οόσsκμ _____

Write the unscrambled words beside their meanings.

a voice _____

an angel _____

a heart _____

a glory _____

a temple _____

a life _____

a place _____

a law _____

a church _____

a truth _____

a peace _____

a house _____

a world _____

a soul _____

☐ Flashcards

144

Greek Workbook - Level 4
Copyright © 1995 by Karen Mohs

Lesson 31

MORE ON FEMININE NOUNS

We have learned about feminine nouns that have
ε, ι, or ρ before the final α. That final α is **_long_**.
We have learned about feminine nouns that have
σ, λλ, ζ, ξ, or ψ before the final α. That final α is **_short_**.

Some feminine nouns end in **η**.

Singular

Nominative	ἡ γραφή	means	**the writing.** (*subject of sentence*)
Genitive	τῆς γραφῆς*	means	**of the writing.** (*shows possession*)
Dative	τῇ γραφῇ*	means	**to (or for) the writing.** (*indirect object*)
Accusative	τὴν γραφήν	means	**the writing.** (*direct object*)
Vocative	γραφή	means	**writing.** (*direct address*)

Write the words under the correct headings.

καρδία	ἡμέρα	δόξα	εἰρήνη	ἐκκλησία	παραβολή
ζωή	ψυχή	ὥρα	βασιλεία	φωνή	ἐντολή

long α in ultima	short α in ultima	η in ultima

*When the ultima is accented, the accent changes to a circumflex in the genitive and dative cases.

☐ Flashcards - (Add the new cards.)

Greek Workbook - Level 4
Copyright © 1995 by Karen Mohs

145

LET'S PRACTICE

Write the meanings of the following Greek words.

γραφή _____   ζωή _____

γραφῆς _____   ζωῆς _____

γραφῇ _____   ζωῇ _____

γραφήν _____   ζωήν _____

γραφή _____   ζωή _____

λίθος _____   δόξα _____

λίθου _____   δόξης _____

λίθῳ _____   δόξῃ _____

λίθον _____   δόξαν _____

λίθε _____   δόξα _____

ὥρα _____   τέκνον _____

ὥρας _____   τέκνου _____

ὥρᾳ _____   τέκνῳ _____

ὥραν _____   τέκνον _____

ὥρα _____   τέκνον _____

☐ Flashcards

146

Greek Workbook - Level 4
Copyright © 1995 by Karen Mohs

LET'S PRACTICE

Choose the correct words for the sentences. Put them in the blanks. Write what the sentences mean.

| ἀλήθεια - ἀλήθειαν |

1. ἡ γραφὴ διδάσκει τὴν _____.

It means _____

| ἐντολὴ - ἐντολῆς |

2. ἡ _____ τοῦ κυρίου φέρει ζωήν.

It means _____

| τέκνον - τέκνῳ |

3. γράφομεν τῷ _____ παραβολὴν τῶν δούλων.

It means _____

| φέρει - φέρουσιν |

4. ἡ φωνὴ τοῦ υἱοῦ _____ τὴν εἰρήνην.

It means _____

| ζωῆς - ζωὴν |

5. ἡ ψυχὴ ἀνθρώπου γινώσκει _____ καὶ θάνατον.

It means _____

| υἱός - υἱοῖς |

6. ἡ ἐκκλησία διδάσκει παραβολὴν τοῖς _____.

It means _____

| δώρῳ - δῶρα |

7. λαμβάνεις τὰ _____· ἀκούεις τὴν ἀλήθειαν.

It means _____

☐ Flashcards

Greek Workbook - Level 4
Copyright © 1995 by Karen Mohs

147

LET'S PRACTICE

Write these sentences in Greek.

1. Brothers and sons hear the commandment.

2. The Scripture teaches the laws of God.

3. You have the truth of the Lord for the world.

4. The child throws stones and destroys houses.

5. The heart knows the glory of the kingdom.

6. I teach a parable; I know the soul.

7. The day of the Lord brings life and peace.

☐ Flashcards

Lesson 32

PLURAL FEMININE NOUNS

The plurals of feminine nouns are all formed in the same way.

Plural

Nom.	αἱ καρδίαι	means	**the hearts.** (*subject of sentence*)
Gen.	τῶν καρδιῶν*	means	**of the hearts.** (*shows possession*)
Dat.	ταῖς καρδίαις	means	**to (or for) the hearts.** (*indirect object*)
Acc.	τὰς καρδίας	means	**the hearts.** (*direct object*)
Voc.	καρδίαι	means	**hearts.** (*direct address*)

Nom.	αἱ δόξαι	means	**the glories.** (*subject of sentence*)
Gen.	τῶν δοξῶν	means	**of the glories.** (*shows possession*)
Dat.	ταῖς δόξαις	means	**to (or for) the glories.** (*indirect object*)
Acc.	τὰς δόξας	means	**the glories.** (*direct object*)
Voc.	δόξαι	means	**glories.** (*direct address*)

Nom.	αἱ γραφαί	means	**the writings.** (*subject of sentence*)
Gen.	τῶν γραφῶν	means	**of the writings.** (*shows possession*)
Dat.	ταῖς γραφαῖς**	means	**to (or for) the writings.** (*indirect object*)
Acc.	τὰς γραφάς	means	**the writings.** (*direct object*)
Voc.	γραφαί	means	**writings.** (*direct address*)

Match the words to their meanings.

τῶν δοξῶν	to the hearts
τὰς βασιλείας	of the glories
ταῖς καρδίαις	the kingdoms

*Plural feminine nouns have a circumflex accent on the ultima in the genitive case (the case that shows possession).
**As we learned with the singular, when the ultima is accented, the accent changes to a circumflex in the genitive and dative cases.

☐ Flashcards - (Add the new cards.)

Greek Workbook - Level 4
Copyright © 1995 by Karen Mohs

149

LET'S PRACTICE

Write the meanings of the following Greek words.

ἡμέραι _____

ἡμερῶν _____

ἡμέραις _____

ἡμέρας _____

ἡμέραι _____

ψυχαί _____

ψυχῶν _____

ψυχαῖς _____

ψυχάς _____

ψυχαί _____

φωναί _____

φωνῶν _____

φωναῖς _____

φωνάς _____

φωναί _____

δόξαι _____

δοξῶν _____

δόξαις _____

δόξας _____

δόξαι _____

οὐρανοί _____

οὐρανῶν _____

οὐρανοῖς _____

οὐρανούς _____

οὐρανοί _____

ὧραι _____

ὡρῶν _____

ὧραις _____

ὧρας _____

ὧραι _____

□ Flashcards

LET'S PRACTICE

Read these Greek sentences. Write what they mean.

1. ἡ φωνὴ τοῦ ἀνθρώπου λέγει τοὺς λόγους τοῦ νόμου.

   It means _____

2. ὁ τόπος τοῦ ἱεροῦ ἔχει οἴκους καὶ λίθους.

   It means _____

3. ἡ παραβολὴ τοῦ κυρίου διδάσκει τὰς ἀληθείας.

   It means _____

4. ὁ κύριος ἐγείρει τὸν υἱὸν καὶ τὸν ἄνθρωπον.

   It means _____

5. ὁ ἀδελφὸς τῶν δούλων ἔχει εἰρήνην.

   It means _____

6. ἀκούω τὰς ἐντολὰς τοῦ θεοῦ· διδάσκω τὸν κόσμον.

   It means _____

7. ἄνθρωποι λύουσι τὸ ἱερόν· ὁ θεὸς ἐγείρει τὸν υἱὸν ἀνθρώπου.

   It means _____

8. τὸ τέκνον βλέπει οὐρανὸν καὶ ἀκούει τὴν φωνὴν τοῦ ἀγγέλου.

   It means _____

9. ἡ ὥρα ἔχει εἰρήνην καὶ ζωήν.

   It means _____

10. διδάσκεις τὴν δόξαν τοῦ θεοῦ· ἀκούεις τοὺς δούλους τῶν υἱῶν.

    It means _____

□ Flashcards

Greek Workbook - Level 4
Copyright © 1995 by Karen Mohs

151

LET'S PRACTICE

Write sentences using the words in the boxes.

1. _____

   It means **I hear voices of angels.**

2. _____

   It means **A child throws stones.**

3. _____

   It means **You have the peace of God.**

4. _____

   It means **We say words to the world.**

ἀγγέλων
τοῦ θεοῦ
λίθους
ἀκούω
λόγους
τὴν εἰρήνην
ἔχετε
τέκνον
τῷ κόσμῳ
φωνὰς
λέγομεν
βάλλει

---

1. _____

   It means **You know the hearts of sons.**

2. _____

   It means **Apostles see kingdoms.**

3. _____

   It means **I write the truth to servants.**

4. _____

   It means **You teach laws of churches.**

βασιλείας
δούλοις
ἀπόστολοι
γράφω
γινώσκετε
ἐκκλησιῶν
υἱῶν
διδάσκεις
τὴν ἀλήθειαν
νόμους
τὰς καρδίας
βλέπουσι

☐ Flashcards

Lesson 33

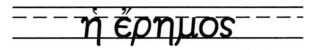

means

the desert

It sounds like hay **e**-ray-mos.

Write the Greek word that means **the desert**.

_____

Match the words to their meanings.

ἡ φωνή	the Scripture
ἡ γραφή	the soul
ἡ ψυχή	the peace
ἡ εἰρήνη	the desert
ἡ ἔρημος	the voice
μένω	I remain
φέρω	I put
βάλλω	I bear
πέμπω	I send
ἡ ἐντολή	the parable
ἡ παραβολή	the commandment
ἡ δόξα	the glory
ἡ ἐκκλησία	the life
ἡ ζωή	the church

☐ Flashcards - (Add the new card.)

Greek Workbook - Level 4
Copyright © 1995 by Karen Mohs

153

LET'S PRACTICE

Write the Greek word that means **the desert**.

Write the Greek words.

the angel

the voice

the brother

the desert

the soul

☐ Flashcards

ἡ ὁδός

means

the road, the way

It sounds like hay ho-**dos**.

Write the Greek word that means **the road** or **the way**.

Circle the words that mean the same as the first words in the rows.

the soul	ἡ ἡμέρα	ἡ ψυχή	τὸ ἱερόν
the peace	ἡ εἰρήνη	ὁ ἀπόστολος	ὁ θεός
the road	ὁ ἄνθρωπος	ἡ ὁδός	ἡ βασιλεία
the life	ἡ ζωή	ἡ ἀλήθεια	ἡ ψυχή
the writing	ἡ ἐντολή	ὁ νόμος	ἡ γραφή
the heart	ἡ καρδία	ὁ θάνατος	ὁ δοῦλος
the desert	ὁ ἄγγελος	ἡ ἔρημος	ὁ κύριος
the church	ὁ κόσμος	ὁ λόγος	ἡ ἐκκλησία
the parable	ἡ παραβολή	ὁ οἶκος	ὁ λίθος
the glory	ὁ ἀδελφός	ὁ οὐρανός	ἡ δόξα
the voice	τὸ τέκνον	ἡ φωνή	ὁ υἱός
the hour	ἡ ὥρα	ὁ τόπος	τὸ δῶρον

☐ Flashcards - (Add the new card.)

Greek Workbook - Level 4
Copyright © 1995 by Karen Mohs

155

LET'S PRACTICE

Write the Greek word that means **the road** or **the way**.

Write the Greek words.

the soul

the way

the law

the desert

the man

☐ Flashcards

LET'S PRACTICE

Write the Greek words.

the heart

the day

the soul

the Scripture

the parable

the truth

the road

the hour

the life

the peace

the glory

the desert

the kingdom

the church

the voice

the commandment

☐ Flashcards

Greek Workbook - Level 4
Copyright © 1995 by Karen Mohs

157

PUZZLE TIME

Find eighteen Greek words in the puzzle below. (Accents and breathing marks have been left off.)

δ	ξ	κ	ε	λ	ν	ψ	υ	χ	η	ο	δ	π	ι	β	α	σ	ι	λ	ε	ι	α
ι	ο	τ	ι	δ	η	γ	ι	ε	ν	τ	ο	λ	η	ο	μ	δ	ν	ρ	γ	ψ	τ
σ	δ	ν	ρ	υ	α	μ	α	ρ	ω	ξ	ξ	η	φ	ε	κ	α	ρ	δ	ι	α	ε
s	ο	μ	η	ρ	ε	θ	ρ	μ	φ	τ	α	φ	α	τ	ζ	χ	ζ	φ	θ	ρ	κ
π	s	χ	ν	σ	ζ	υ	γ	s	ε	ο	φ	α	π	δ	τ	κ	ω	η	ρ	ε	ν
β	ω	θ	η	ψ	α	β	ω	ζ	χ	π	α	ρ	α	β	ο	λ	η	β	μ	μ	ο
υ	ε	ο	κ	λ	ι	κ	ξ	α	π	ο	s	γ	ψ	λ	γ	λ	ξ	ε	ν	η	ν
ε	κ	κ	λ	η	σ	ι	α	ζ	η	s	θ	σ	α	ι	ε	θ	η	λ	α	ρ	β

Write the words you found. Remember to add the breathing marks and accents.

1. _____

2. _____

3. _____

4. _____

5. _____

6. _____

7. _____

8. _____

9. _____

10. _____

11. _____

12. _____

13. _____

14. _____

15. _____

16. _____

17. _____

18. _____

☐ Flashcards

Lesson 34

MORE ON FEMININE NOUNS

We learned that words ending in **os** are usually masculine.
For example, ὁ ἄνθρωπος is masculine.

Now we know two words ending in **os** that are feminine.
ἡ ὁδός and ἡ ἔρημος

Their forms are like the masculine nouns ending in **os**.

Singular

Nom.	ἡ ὁδός	means	**the road.** (*subject of sentence*)
Gen.	τῆς ὁδοῦ	means	**of the road.** (*shows possession*)
Dat.	τῇ ὁδῷ	means	**to (or for) the road.** (*indirect object*)
Acc.	τὴν ὁδόν	means	**the road.** (*direct object*)
Voc.	ὁδέ	means	**road.** (*direct address*)

Plural

Nom.	αἱ ὁδοί	means	**the roads.** (*subject of sentence*)
Gen.	τῶν ὁδῶν	means	**of the roads.** (*shows possession*)
Dat.	ταῖς ὁδοῖς	means	**to (or for) the roads.** (*indirect object*)
Acc.	τὰς ὁδούς	means	**the roads.** (*direct object*)
Voc.	ὁδοί	means	**roads.** (*direct address*)

Circle the correct words.

the road	the desert	to the road
ὁ ὁδός ἡ ὁδός τὸ ὁδός	τὸ ἔρημον τὸν ἔρημον τὴν ἔρημον	τῇ ὁδῷ τῷ ὁδῷ τοῖς ὁδῷ
for the deserts	the roads	of the desert
τοῖς ἐρήμοις τῇ ἐρήμοις ταῖς ἐρήμοις	τὰ ὁδούς τοὺς ὁδούς τὰς ὁδούς	τοῦ ἐρήμου τῆς ἐρήμου τῶν ἐρήμου

☐ Flashcards - (Add the new cards.)

Greek Workbook - Level 4
Copyright © 1995 by Karen Mohs

LET'S PRACTICE

Match the letters of the Greek sentences to their meanings below.

a. λαμβάνω τὴν ὁδὸν ζωῆς· λαμβάνει τὴν ὁδὸν θανάτου.

b. ἡ φωνὴ τοῦ ἀγγέλου ἄγει τὴν ψυχὴν τοῦ ἀνθρώπου.

c. βλέπεις τὴν ἔρημον· γινώσκεις τὴν ἀλήθειαν τῆς βασιλείας.

d. πέμπω τὰ δῶρα· διδάσκει τοὺς λόγους τοῦ κυρίου.

e. ὁ ἀπόστολος γράφει τὰς γραφὰς ταῖς ἐκκλησίαις θεοῦ.

f. ἡ δόξα τοῦ κυρίου φέρει εἰρήνην καὶ ζωήν.

g. λέγομεν παραβολὰς τοῖς ἀδελφοῖς καὶ τοῖς υἱοῖς ἀδελφῶν.

h. αἱ ἐντολαὶ τοῦ θεοῦ φέρουσι ζωήν· γινώσκει τὰς ψυχάς.

i. ὁ κόσμος λύει τὴν εἰρήνην· ἔχομεν τὴν εἰρήνην θεοῦ.

( )　1. I send the gifts; he teaches the words of the Lord.

( )　2. God's commandments bring life; He knows the souls.

( )　3. The glory of the Lord brings peace and life.

( )　4. The world destroys the peace; we have the peace of God.

( )　5. I take the way of life; he takes the way of death.

( )　6. You see the desert; you know the truth of the kingdom.

( )　7. We say parables to the brothers and to the sons of brothers.

( )　8. The voice of the angel leads the man's soul.

( )　9. The apostle writes the Scriptures for the churches of God.

☐ Flashcards

160

Lesson 35

FINAL REVIEW

Write the meanings of the following Greek words.

μένω _____

ἱερόν _____

ψυχή _____

ἀλήθεια _____

γράφω _____

κόσμος _____

λύω _____

εἰρήνη _____

ἐκκλησία _____

ἀκούω _____

ἀπόστολος _____

λίθος _____

λαμβάνω _____

καρδία _____

ἐγείρω _____

νόμος _____

ὁδός _____

πέμπω _____

οὐρανός _____

υἱός _____

δόξα _____

λέγω _____

βασιλεία _____

γινώσκω _____

παραβολή _____

ζωή _____

ἔχω _____

οἶκος _____

ὥρα _____

θάνατος _____

ἄνθρωπος _____

ἐντολή _____

γραφή _____

διδάσκω _____

τέκνον _____

ἔρημος _____

βάλλω _____

δοῦλος _____

φέρω _____

ἀδελφός _____

κύριος _____

φωνή _____

δῶρον _____

θεός _____

ἡμέρα _____

βλέπω _____

τόπος _____

ἄγγελος _____

ἄγω _____

λόγος _____

☐ Flashcards

Greek Workbook - Level 4
Copyright © 1995 by Karen Mohs

161

FINAL REVIEW

Write the correct articles for these Greek words.

δῶρα	ἐκκλησίας	ἀδελφοί
τόπον	δώρῳ	ἐντολῶν
παραβολῆς	καρδίαν	ἀληθείᾳ
λίθοις	ζωή	δόξα
δοξῶν	ἱεροῦ	υἱῷ
βασιλεία	ἔρημος	ἐκκλησίαι
δοῦλος	τόπους	οὐρανοῦ
ἀλήθειαι	ἐντολήν	ὁδόν
ὁδοῦ	ὁδῶν	ἡμέρας
παραβολαῖς	τέκνον	ἐρήμοις
καρδιῶν	ἐκκλησίαις	ψυχῇ
ἐρήμῳ	ἀληθείαις	δώροις
ψυχάς	δόξῃ	δόξαις
ἐκκλησίαν	ἀποστόλων	τέκνων
ἱερά	ἐρήμους	ὁδοί
γραφαί	ὥρας	τόπου

☐ Flashcards

162

Greek Workbook - Level 4
Copyright © 1995 by Karen Mohs

FINAL REVIEW

Label the three final Greek syllables.

λαμ   βά   νο   μεν

_____ _____ _____ _____

Accent the following verbs according to the rules of accent. Add breathing marks where needed.

λεγεις	ακουεις	γραφω
μενει	βλεπομεν	βαλλομεν
ακουουσι	εγειρει	λαμβανετε
γινωσκομεν	εχετε	πεμπω
φερετε	λαμβανουσι	γινωσκει
αγουσι	διδασκεις	λυω

Accent the following nouns according to the rules of accent. Add breathing marks where needed. (The first word in each row shows where the accent starts.) (Hint: Remember the genitive plural rule at the bottom of page 149.)

(βασιλεία)	βασιλειαι	βασιλεια	βασιλειαν
(ἐντολή)	εντολης	εντολαις	εντολας
(δόξα)	δοξαι	δοξας	δοξων
(ἀλήθεια)	αληθειων	αληθειαις	αληθειας
(παραβολή)	παραβολην	παραβολας	παραβολη
(ἐκκλησία)	εκκλησιας	εκκλησιων	εκκλησια
(ἡμέρα)	ημερας	ημερα	ημεραν

☐ Flashcards

Greek Workbook - Level 4
Copyright © 1995 by Karen Mohs

FINAL REVIEW

Circle the correct meanings of the Greek sentences.

ἡ ἔρημος μένει.	The desert remains. A desert remains. Deserts remain.
ἀκούομεν τὴν φωνὴν τοῦ τέκνου.	We hear the child's voice. You hear a child's voice. We hear a child's voice.
ὁ ἀδελφὸς βλέπει τὰς ὁδούς.	The brother sees the road. The brothers see the road. The brother sees the roads.
ἡ καρδία γινώσκει τὴν ἀλήθειαν.	The heart knows the truth. A heart knows the truth. Heart, know the truth.
λύουσι τὸν τόπον.	He destroys the place. They destroy the place. They destroy the places.
ὁ ἄνθρωπος ἄγει τὴν ἐκκλησίαν.	A man leads a church. A man leads the church. The man leads the church.
βάλλομεν τοὺς λίθους.	We throw the stones. We throw stones. You throw the stones.
γράφει τοὺς λόγους θεοῦ.	He writes the words of God. He writes words to God. He writes the words to God.

Flashcards

164

Greek Workbook - Level 4
Copyright © 1995 by Karen Mohs

FINAL REVIEW

Write the meanings beside the Greek words.

Verbs

ἀκούω _____   ἀκούομεν _____

ἀκούεις _____   ἀκούετε _____

ἀκούει _____   ἀκούουσι _____

Masculine (2nd declension) nouns

ὁ λίθος _____   οἱ λίθοι _____

τοῦ λίθου _____   τῶν λίθων _____

τῷ λίθῳ _____   τοῖς λίθοις _____

τὸν λίθον _____   τοὺς λίθους _____

λίθε _____   λίθοι _____

Verbs

λαμβάνω _____   λαμβάνομεν _____

λαμβάνεις _____   λαμβάνετε _____

λαμβάνει _____   λαμβάνουσι _____

Neuter (2nd declension) nouns

τὸ τέκνον _____   τὰ τέκνα _____

τοῦ τέκνου _____   τῶν τέκνων _____

τῷ τέκνῳ _____   τοῖς τέκνοις _____

τὸ τέκνον _____   τὰ τέκνα _____

τέκνον _____   τέκνα _____

☐ Flashcards

Greek Workbook - Level 4
Copyright © 1995 by Karen Mohs

165

Lesson 36

FINAL REVIEW

Write the meanings beside the Greek words.

Verbs

ἔχω _____   ἔχομεν _____

ἔχεις _____   ἔχετε _____

ἔχει _____   ἔχουσι _____

Feminine (1st declension) nouns ending in long α

ἡ ἡμέρα _____   αἱ ἡμέραι _____

τῆς ἡμέρας _____   τῶν ἡμερῶν _____

τῇ ἡμέρᾳ _____   ταῖς ἡμέραις _____

τὴν ἡμέραν _____   τὰς ἡμέρας _____

ἡμέρα _____   ἡμέραι _____

Verbs

λέγω _____   λέγομεν _____

λέγεις _____   λέγετε _____

λέγει _____   λέγουσι _____

Feminine (1st declension) nouns ending in short α

ἡ δόξα _____   αἱ δόξαι _____

τῆς δόξης _____   τῶν δοξῶν _____

τῇ δόξῃ _____   ταῖς δόξαις _____

τὴν δόξαν _____   τὰς δόξας _____

δόξα _____   δόξαι _____

☐ Flashcards

FINAL REVIEW

Write the meanings beside the Greek words.

Verbs

γινώσκω _____　　γινώσκομεν _____

γινώσκεις _____　　γινώσκετε _____

γινώσκει _____　　γινώσκουσι _____

Feminine (1st declension) nouns ending in η

ἡ ψυχή _____　　αἱ ψυχαί _____

τῆς ψυχῆς _____　　τῶν ψυχῶν _____

τῇ ψυχῇ _____　　ταῖς ψυχαῖς _____

τὴν ψυχήν _____　　τὰς ψυχάς _____

ψυχή _____　　ψυχαί _____

Verbs

βλέπω _____　　βλέπομεν _____

βλέπεις _____　　βλέπετε _____

βλέπει _____　　βλέπουσι _____

Feminine nouns of the 2nd declension

ἡ ἔρημος _____　　αἱ ἔρημοι _____

τῆς ἐρήμου _____　　τῶν ἐρημῶν _____

τῇ ἐρήμῳ _____　　ταῖς ἐρήμοις _____

τὴν ἔρημον _____　　τὰς ἐρήμους _____

ἔρημε _____　　ἔρημοι _____

☐ Flashcards

Greek Workbook - Level 4
Copyright © 1995 by Karen Mohs

FINAL REVIEW

Write these sentences in Greek.

1. The men and the brothers say words.

2. You (sing.) say to the son and to the slave the truth.

3. The house and the temple and the kingdom remain.

4. Sons, you see the stones of the temple.

5. We write the laws for the children.

6. The sons of God know life and truth.

7. Lord, we know the glory of the heart of God.

☐ Flashcards

FINAL REVIEW

Read these Greek sentences. Write what they mean.

1. λαμβάνεις τοὺς οἴκους τῶν ἀνθρώπων καὶ τῶν ἀποστόλων.

   It means _____

2. οἱ ἄγγελοι οὐρανοῦ λέγουσι τοὺς λόγους καὶ διδάσκουσιν εἰρήνην.

   It means _____

3. ἡ ὁδὸς τῆς ἐρήμου ἄγει τοὺς υἱοὺς καὶ τοὺς ἀδελφούς.

   It means _____

4. οἱ ἀπόστολοι φέρουσι τὰς γραφὰς τοῦ θεοῦ· γινώσκουσι ζωήν.

   It means _____

5. ἡ καρδία καὶ ἡ ψυχὴ ἀνθρώπου ἀκούουσι τοὺς λόγους ζωῆς.

   It means _____

6. ἀδελφοί, ἀκούετε τὴν φωνὴν καὶ γινώσκετε τὰς ἐντολάς.

   It means _____

7. ἡ παραβολὴ τῶν δούλων διδάσκει τὴν ἀλήθειαν.

   It means _____

8. βάλλουσι λίθους· γράφω τοὺς νόμους τοῦ κόσμου.

   It means _____

9. αἱ ἐκκλησίαι τοῦ θεοῦ γινώσκουσι τὴν δόξαν τοῦ θεοῦ.

   It means _____

10. ἡ ἀλήθεια διδάσκει υἱοὺς καὶ τὰς καρδίας ἀνθρώπων.

    It means _____

□ Flashcards

Greek Workbook - Level 4
Copyright © 1995 by Karen Mohs

169

PUZZLE TIME

Think of the meanings of the English words. Write the Greek words on the puzzle below. (Do not include the accents or the breathing marks.)

across

1. I see
5. a kingdom
9. a death
11. a desert
12. a parable
13. a road
15. I teach
17. a brother
23. a heart
24. I raise up
26. a church
28. I destroy
29. a day
30. a servant
32. a Scripture
33. I know
36. a law
37. an angel
38. a house
41. an apostle
42. a commandment
43. a temple
44. I bring
45. an hour

down

2. I take
3. a place
4. a gift
6. a truth
7. I have
8. I hear
9. God
10. a glory
14. I send
16. a world
18. a voice
19. I write
20. I throw
21. a child
22. a heaven
23. a lord
25. a peace
27. a word
31. I say
34. a soul
35. a son
39. and
40. I remain
41. I lead

☐ Flashcards

170

Greek Workbook - Level 4
Copyright © 1995 by Karen Mohs

APPENDIX

Greek - English Glossary

α
ἄγγελος, ὁ - an angel (13)
ἅγιος, -α, -ον - *adj.*, holy
ἄγω - I lead (43)
ἀδελφός, ὁ - a brother (7)
ἀκούω - *(can take gen. or acc. case object)* I hear (15)
ἀλήθεια, ἡ - a truth, truth (101)
ἄνθρωπος, ὁ - a man (7)
ἀπόστολος, ὁ - an apostle (7)

β
βάλλω - I throw, I cast, I put (61)
βασιλεία, ἡ - a kingdom (103)
βλέπω - I see (7)

γ
γινώσκω - I know (9)
γράμμα, τό - a letter
γραφή, ἡ - a writing, a Scripture (129)
γράφω - I write (11)
γυνή, ἡ - a woman

δ
διδάσκω - I teach (11)
δόξα, ἡ - a glory, glory (121)
δοῦλος, ὁ - a slave, a servant (9)
δῶρον, τό - a gift (15)

ε
ἔβαλον - a form of βάλλω
ἐγείρω - I raise up (39)
εἶδον - a form of ὁράω
εἰμί - I am
εἶπον - a form of λέγω
εἰρήνη, ἡ - a peace, peace (131)
εἰς - into

εἷς - one
ἐκ - out of
ἐκκλησία, ἡ - a church (111)
ἐντολή, ἡ - a commandment (133)
ἐξ - a form of ἐκ
ἑπτά - seven
ἔρημος, ἡ - a desert (153)
ἔσομαι - a form of εἰμί
ἔχω - I have (13)

ζ
ζάω - I live
ζωή, ἡ - a life, life (135)

η
ἡ - the (feminine article) (101, 149)
ἡμέρα, ἡ - a day (105)
ἤχθη - a form of ἄγω

θ
θάνατος, ὁ - a death, death (41)
θεός, ὁ - God, a god (37)

ι
ἰδού - behold! lo!
ἰδών - a form of ὁράω
ἱερόν, τό - a temple (15)
ἵνα - in order that

κ
καί - *conj.*, and (9)
καρδία, ἡ - a heart (107)
κόσμος, ὁ - a world (45)
κύριος, ὁ - Lord, a lord (33)

λ
λαμβάνω - I take (15)
λέγω - I say (13)

λίθος, ὁ - a stone (59)
λόγος, ὁ - a word (9)
λύω - I loose, I destroy (35)

μ
μείζων - greater
μένω - I remain, I abide (65)
μηδείς - no one, nothing

ν
νόμος, ὁ - a law (13)

ο
ὁ - the (masculine article) (49, 51)
ὁδός, ἡ - a way, a road (155)
οἶδα - I know
οἶκος, ὁ - a house (11)
ὄρος, τό - a mountain
οὖν - *conj.*, *postpositive*, accordingly, therefore
οὐρανός, ὁ - a heaven, heaven (63)
οὖσα - a form of εἰμί
ὄχλος, ὁ - a crowd, a multitude

π
παραβολή, ἡ - a parable (137)
πέμπω - I send (69)
πίστις, ἡ - faith
πλείων - more
ποῖος - what sort of?
πούς, ὁ - a foot

ρ
ῥακά - worthless fellow

σ
σάρξ, ἡ - flesh
σπείρω - I sow

Note: The number in parentheses indicates the page on which the vocabulary word is introduced.

Greek Workbook - Level 4
Copyright © 1995 by Karen Mohs

171

APPENDIX

Greek - English Glossary

Τ

τέκνον, τό - a child (67)

τηρέω - I keep

τό - the (neuter article) (55)

τόπος, ὁ - a place (71)

υ

υἱός, ὁ - a son (11)

φ

φέρω - I bear, I bring (73)

φωνή, ἡ - a voice (139)

χ

χάρις, ἡ - grace

χείρ, ἡ - a hand

ψ

ψυχή, ἡ - a soul (141)

ω

ὥρα, ἡ - an hour (109)

ὤφθην - a form of ὁράω

APPENDIX

English - Greek Glossary

a
accordingly - οὖν
and - καί
angel - ἄγγελος, ὁ
apostle - ἀπόστολος, ὁ

b
bear - φέρω
bring - φέρω
brother - ἀδελφός, ὁ

c
cast - βάλλω
child - τέκνον, τό
church - ἐκκλησία, ἡ
commandment - ἐντολή, ἡ

d
day - ἡμέρα, ἡ
death - θάνατος, ὁ
desert - ἔρημος, ἡ
destroy - λύω

g
gift - δῶρον, τό
glory - δόξα, ἡ
God - θεός, ὁ
god - θεός, ὁ

h
have - ἔχω
hear - ἀκούω
heart - καρδία, ἡ
heaven - οὐρανός, ὁ
hour - ὥρα, ἡ
house - οἶκος, ὁ

k
kingdom - βασιλεία, ἡ
know - γινώσκω

l
law - νόμος, ὁ
lead - ἄγω
life - ζωή, ἡ
loose - λύω
Lord - κύριος, ὁ
lord - κύριος, ὁ

m
man - ἄνθρωπος, ὁ

p
parable - παραβολή, ἡ
peace - εἰρήνη, ἡ
place - τόπος, ὁ
put - βάλλω

r
raise up - ἐγείρω
remain - μένω
road - ὁδός, ἡ

s
say - λέγω
Scripture - γραφή, ἡ
see - βλέπω
send - πέμπω
servant - δοῦλος, ὁ
slave - δοῦλος, ὁ
son - υἱός, ὁ
soul - ψυχή, ἡ
stone - λίθος, ὁ

t
take - λαμβάνω
teach - διδάσκω
temple - ἱερόν, τό
the - ὁ, ἡ, τό
therefore - οὖν
throw - βάλλω
truth - ἀλήθεια, ἡ

v
voice - φωνή, ἡ

w
way - ὁδός, ἡ
word - λόγος, ὁ
world - κόσμος, ὁ
write - γράφω
writing - γραφή, ἡ

Greek Workbook - Level 4
Copyright © 1995 by Karen Mohs

174

Greek Workbook - Level 4
Copyright © 1995 by Karen Mohs

APPENDIX

Greek Alphabet

Capital Letter	Small Letter	Name	Pronunciation	Capital Letter	Small Letter	Name	Pronunciation
A	α	alpha (**al**-fa)	**a** in *father*	N	ν	nu (noo)	**n** in *nice*
B	β	beta (**bay**-ta)	**b** in *bat*	Ξ	ξ	xi (ksee)	**x** in *box*
Γ	γ	gamma (**gam**-ma)	**g** in *God*	O	o	omicron (**ahm**-i-cron)	**o** in *obey**
Δ	δ	delta (**del**-ta)	**d** in *dog*	Π	π	pi (pie)	**p** in *pie*
E	ε	epsilon (**ep**-si-lon)	**e** in *get*	P	ρ	rho (row)	**r** in *row*
Z	ζ	zeta (**zay**-ta)	**dz** in *adze*	Σ	σ ς	sigma (**sig**-ma)	**s** in *sit*
H	η	eta (**ay**-ta)	**a** in *late*	T	τ	tau (tou)	**t** in *toy*
Θ	θ	theta (**thay**-ta)	**th** in *bath*	Υ	υ	upsilon (**up**-si-lon)	**oo** in *good*
I	ι	iota (ee-**o**-ta)	**i** in *pit*	Φ	φ	phi (fee)	**f** in *fun*
K	κ	kappa (**kap**-pa)	**k** in *kite*	X	χ	chi (kee)	**ch** in *Ach*
Λ	λ	lambda (**lamb**-da)	**l** in *lamb*	Ψ	ψ	psi (psee)	**ps** in *lips*
M	μ	mu (moo)	**m** in *man*	Ω	ω	omega (o-**may**-ga)	**o** in *note**

*The o and the ω both have a long o sound, but the ω is held longer.

Vowels and Diphthongs

Short Vowels:

α	**a** in *father*
ε	**e** in *get*
o	**o** in *obey*
ι	**i** in *pit*
υ	**oo** in *good*

Long Vowels:

α	**a** in *father*, but held longer
η	**a** in *late*
ω	**o** in *note*
ι	**ee** in *feet*
υ	**oo** in *good*, but held longer

Most common Greek diphthongs:

αι	**ai** in *aisle*
ει	**a** in *fate* (same sound as η)
οι	**oi** in *oil*
αυ	**ow** in *cow*
ευ	**eu** in *feud*
ου	**oo** in *food*
υι	**uee** in *queen*

(Note: A diphthong combines two vowels into one syllable. For example, the **oi** in our English word **boil** is a diphthong.)

When an iota (ι) follows certain long vowels (α, η, ω), it is written below the letter instead of after it (ᾳ, ῃ, ῳ). This is called an **iota subscript**. These diphthongs sound the same as the long vowels alone.

Greek Workbook - Level 4
Copyright © 1995 by Karen Mohs

175

APPENDIX

Punctuation

Greek punctuation marks:

1. The comma (,)
   It is used like our English comma.

2. The colon (·)
   This looks like the top half of our English colon. It is used like our English colon and our English semicolon.

3. The period (.)
   It is used like our English period.

4. The question mark (;)
   This looks like our English semicolon, but it is really a Greek question mark.

Breathing Marks

If a vowel or a diphthong begins a word, it always has a **breathing mark** placed directly above it. (On a diphthong, the breathing mark is on the second vowel.)

rough (‛)
ἑν sounds like *hen*

smooth (’)
ἐν sounds like *en*

(Note: Whenever the consonant ρ begins a word, it has a rough breathing mark.)

Word Order

The usual order of words in the Greek sentence is like the English sentence.

SUBJECT - VERB - DIRECT OBJECT

However, if you want to call attention to a certain word or phrase, put it at the beginning of the sentence. You may also change the order of words to make the sentence sound better.

APPENDIX

Syllables

The last three syllables of Greek words are named as follows:

1. The last syllable is the **ultima**.
2. The syllable before the ultima is the **penult**.
3. The syllable before the penult is the **antepenult**.

$$\underset{\text{antepenult}}{\overset{.}{\alpha}} \quad \underset{\text{penult}}{\pi\acute{o}} \quad \underset{}{\sigma\tau o} \quad \underset{\text{ultima}}{\lambda os}$$

Long syllables:

1. A syllable is long if it contains a long vowel.
   Example: πω in βλέπω is a long syllable.

2. A syllable is long if it contains a diphthong (except αι or οι at the end of a word).
   Example: δοῦ in δοῦλος is a long syllable.

Short syllables:

1. A syllable is short if it contains a short vowel.
   Example: γος in λόγος is a short syllable.

2. A syllable is short if it contains αι or οι (at the end of a word).
   Example: φοί in ἀδελφοί is a short syllable.
   BUT   φοῖς in ἀδελφοῖς is a long syllable because a letter (ς) comes after the οι.

Accents

The three Greek accents:

1. The acute accent (´)
2. The circumflex accent (⌢)
3. The grave accent (`)

An accent only stands over vowels. If a vowel is part of a diphthong, the accent stands over the second vowel of the pair. If a breathing mark and an acute accent stand over the same vowel, the breathing mark is always first. (ἄγω) If a breathing mark and a circumflex accent stand over the same vowel, the circumflex accent is placed over the breathing mark. (οἶκος)

(Note: In ancient times, the three accents were used to show musical pitch, not stress. Since today we cannot know the musical pitch used in those ancient times, we use the accent simply to show which syllable to stress when pronouncing a word.)

Greek Workbook - Level 4
Copyright © 1995 by Karen Mohs

177

APPENDIX

Rules of Accent

I. General Rules

A. The Acute Accent
1. The acute accent (´) can stand only on one of the last three syllables.
2. The acute accent (´) can stand on long or short syllables.
3. When the ultima is long, the acute accent (´) cannot stand on the antepenult.
4. When the ultima is short, the acute accent (´) cannot stand on a long penult.

B. The Circumflex Accent
1. The circumflex accent (⌢) can stand only on one of the last two syllables.
2. The circumflex accent (⌢) can stand only on long syllables.
3. When the ultima is long, the circumflex accent (⌢) cannot stand on the penult.
4. When the ultima is short and the penult is long and is accented, the accent must be a circumflex (⌢).

C. The Grave Accent
1. The grave accent (`) can stand only on the last syllable.
2. When a word has an acute accent on its last syllable and it is followed immediately by another word, the acute accent is changed to a grave accent (`).

II. Specific Rules

A. Rule of Verb Accent
The accent on a verb wants to be as close to the front of the word as it can.
   a. If the ultima is short, accent the antepenult. (If there is no antepenult, accent the penult.)
   b. If the ultima is long, accent the penult.

B. Rule of Noun Accent
The accent on a noun wants to stay where it is. Sometimes it has to move because of the general accent rules.
   a. Sometimes the accent can stay where it started.
   b. Sometimes it stays where it started, but it must change form.
   c. Sometimes it must move to another syllable, but it always wants to get back to the place it started.

(Note: In nouns with an acute accent on the ultima [like υἱός], when the ultima becomes long, the acute changes to a circumflex except in the accusative plural.)

APPENDIX

Moods of the Greek Verb

Greek verbs are classified according to mood.

> The **indicative** *mood* is used to make an assertion.
> The **subjunctive** *mood* is used to express a possibility.
> The **imperative** *mood* is used to make a command.
> The **optative** *mood* (rarely used in the Greek New Testament) is used to express a wish.

A **participle** is a verbal adjective, and an **infinitive** is a verbal noun.

Voices of the Greek Verb

Voices of the Greek verb:

> **Active Voice:** The subject of the sentence is *doing an action*.
> > Example: The man loves the woman.
>
> **Middle Voice:** The subject of the sentence is *doing an action that in some way concerns itself*.
> > Example: The man loves himself.
>
> **Passive Voice:** The subject of the sentence is *receiving an action*.
> > Example: The man is being loved by the woman.

Present Tense

The *present tense* is used to describe **continuous** action. In the *indicative mood*, the action occurs in the **present** time and can be either **continuous** or the length of the action can be unknown (**undefined**). A **moveable** *ν* stands on some present tense forms.

Present Active Indicative
(present system verb stem + variable vowel + primary active ending)

	Singular	Meaning	Plural	Meaning
1st Person	βλέπω	I see	βλέπομεν	we see
2nd Person	βλέπεις	you (s.) see	βλέπετε	you (pl.) see
3rd Person	βλέπει	he (she, it) sees	βλέπουσι(ν)	they see

Greek Workbook - Level 4
Copyright © 1995 by Karen Mohs

APPENDIX

The Article

Greek has no indefinite article. A Greek noun **without** the article is usually translated with our English indefinite article (*a* or *an*). (For example, λόγος means *a word*.) A Greek noun **with** the article is usually translated with our English definite article (*the*). (For example, ὁ λόγος means *the word*.) Articles agree with the nouns they modify in gender, number, and case.

	Singular Masculine	*Singular* Feminine	*Singular* Neuter	*Plural* Masculine	*Plural* Feminine	*Plural* Neuter
Nominative	ὁ	ἡ	τό	οἱ	αἱ	τά
Genitive	τοῦ	τῆς	τοῦ	τῶν	τῶν	τῶν
Dative	τῷ	τῇ	τῷ	τοῖς	ταῖς	τοῖς
Accusative	τόν	τήν	τό	τούς	τάς	τά

The articles ὁ, ἡ, οἱ, and αἱ are proclitics.

Gender of the Greek Noun

The three genders of Greek nouns are masculine, feminine, and neuter.

Cases of the Greek Noun

Greek nouns are classified into five *cases*.

The subject of the sentence belongs in the **nominative** case. Possession is expressed with the **genitive** case. The indirect object belongs in the **dative** case. The direct object belongs in the **accusative** case. Nouns of direct address belong in the **vocative** case. These cases have other important uses as well.

APPENDIX

First Declension

All nouns of the first declension ending in -α or -η are feminine.

Every first declension noun has a circumflex on the ultima in the genitive plural, no matter where the accent started. The final α in three of the singular cases (nominative, genitive, and accusative) and in one of the plural cases (accusative) is long. (An exception to this rule is ἀλήθεια. In this word, the final α is short in the nominative and accusative singular.)

In first and second declension nouns with an accented ultima, the genitive and dative singular and plural must have a circumflex accent. In these nouns, the accusative plural must have an acute accent.

First Declension - Long α

In feminine nouns ending in -α preceded by ε, ι, or ρ, that final α is *long*.

	Singular	Meaning	Plural	Meaning
Nominative	ἡ καρδία	the heart	αἱ καρδίαι	the hearts
Genitive	τῆς καρδίας	of the heart	τῶν καρδιῶν	of the hearts
Dative	τῇ καρδίᾳ	to/for the heart	ταῖς καρδίαις	to/for the hearts
Accusative	τὴν καρδίαν	the heart	τὰς καρδίας	the hearts
Vocative	καρδία	heart	καρδίαι	hearts

First Declension - Short α

In feminine nouns ending in -α preceded by σ, λλ, ζ, ξ, or ψ, that final α is *short*. It changes to an η in the genitive and dative singular.

	Singular	Meaning	Plural	Meaning
Nominative	ἡ δόξα	(the) glory	αἱ δόξαι	(the) glories
Genitive	τῆς δόξης	of (the) glory	τῶν δοξῶν	of (the) glories
Dative	τῇ δόξῃ	to/for (the) glory	ταῖς δόξαις	to/for (the) glories
Accusative	τὴν δόξαν	(the) glory	τὰς δόξας	(the) glories
Vocative	δόξα	glory	δόξαι	glories

APPENDIX

First Declension (continued)

First Declension - η

In feminine nouns ending in -η, the η is retained throughout the singular.

	Singular	*Meaning*	*Plural*	*Meaning*
Nominative	ἡ φωνή	the voice	αἱ φωναί	the voices
Genitive	τῆς φωνῆς	of the voice	τῶν φωνῶν	of the voices
Dative	τῇ φωνῇ	to/for the voice	ταῖς φωναῖς	to/for the voices
Accusative	τὴν φωνήν	the voice	τὰς φωνάς	the voices
Vocative	φωνή	voice	φωναί	voices

APPENDIX

Second Declension

In first and second declension nouns with an accented ultima, the genitive and dative singular and plural must have a circumflex accent. In these nouns, the accusative plural must have an acute accent.

Second Declension - Masculine

Most nouns of the second declension ending in -*os* are masculine.

	Singular	*Meaning*	*Plural*	*Meaning*
Nominative	ὁ ἀδελφός	the brother	οἱ ἀδελφοί	the brothers
Genitive	τοῦ ἀδελφοῦ	of the brother	τῶν ἀδελφῶν	of the brothers
Dative	τῷ ἀδελφῷ	to/for the brother	τοῖς ἀδελφοῖς	to/for the brothers
Accusative	τὸν ἀδελφόν	the brother	τοὺς ἀδελφούς	the brothers
Vocative	ἀδελφέ	brother	ἀδελφοί	brothers

Second Declension - Feminine

Nearly all nouns of the second declension ending in -*os* are masculine. However, certain words, such as ἔρημος and ὁδός are feminine.

Nominative	ἡ ὁδός	the road	αἱ ὁδοί	the roads
Genitive	τῆς ὁδοῦ	of the road	τῶν ὁδῶν	of the roads
Dative	τῇ ὁδῷ	to/for the road	ταῖς ὁδοῖς	to/for the roads
Accusative	τὴν ὁδόν	the road	τὰς ὁδούς	the roads
Vocative	ὁδέ	road	ὁδοί	roads

Second Declension - Neuter

All nouns of the second declension ending in -*ov* are neuter.

Nominative	τὸ δῶρον	the gift	τὰ δῶρα	the gifts
Genitive	τοῦ δώρου	of the gift	τῶν δώρων	of the gifts
Dative	τῷ δώρῳ	to/for the gift	τοῖς δώροις	to/for the gifts
Accusative	τὸ δῶρον	the gift	τὰ δῶρα	the gifts
Vocative	δῶρον	gift	δῶρα	gifts

Greek Workbook - Level 4
Copyright © 1995 by Karen Mohs

APPENDIX

Bible Copy Work

Materials needed:

1. A Greek interlinear version of the New Testament. (These are available through local Christian bookstores as well as through many catalog and internet companies.)

2. A blank journal containing lined pages. (Notebook paper in a loose-leaf binder or a spiral notebook will work just as well.)

Assignment:

1. Copy work should take no more than five or ten minutes daily. A young student will begin copying one word a session. With maturity and with increased understanding of koiné Greek, he will advance to phrases and eventually to entire verses.

2. Keep the focus on understanding. Simply forming the letters as the mind wanders here and there is unproductive.

3. Bear in mind that consistent daily work in small doses is much more profitable than infrequent longer sessions.

Procedure:

1. Begin with the Gospel of John. (An alternate suggestion would be to begin with the Gospel of Matthew and progress through the books of the New Testament. However, especially for younger students, we recommend beginning in John.)

2. Write the name of the book and the chapter number (e.g. "John Chapter 1") centered on the first line.

3. Skip the next line.

4. On the third line, write the verse number. Begin copying the Greek words, including all accents, breathing marks, and punctuation marks.

5. At the end of that third line, skip a line and continue copying the Greek words, always skipping a line between each line of Greek text.

6. Now go back to the beginning and write the English meaning beneath the Greek words as shown in the Greek interlinear.

184

Greek Workbook - Level 4
Copyright © 1995 by Karen Mohs

APPENDIX

Index

accents, named, 80; position, 80; placement in relation to breathing mark, 80; purpose, 80; general rules, 85-91; rules of verb accent, 93; rules of noun accent, 95; change to circumflex on genitive and dative cases in first and second declensions, 95; circumflex on first declension genitive plural nouns, 149; See appendix page 177, 178.

accusative case, common use, 20; use demonstrated, 20; See appendix page 180.

acute accent, 85; and breathing mark, 80; See appendix page 177, 178.

alphabet, 1-5; See appendix page 175.

antepenult, 81; See appendix page 177.

article, use demonstrated, 8; masculine singular, 49; masculine plural, 51; neuter, 55; feminine, 115, 117; See appendix page 180.

Bible copy work, See appendix page 184.

breathing marks, 79, 80; See appendix page 176.

case endings, second declension masculine nouns, 20-25; second declension neuter nouns, 30; first declension long alpha nouns, 117; first declension short alpha nouns, 125; first declension eta nouns, 145; first declension plural nouns, 149; second declension feminine nouns, 159; See appendix pages 181-183.

circumflex accent, 87; and breathing marks, 80; genitive and dative cases in first and second declensions, 95; first declension genitive plural nouns, 149; See appendix page 177, 178, 181, 183.

colon, 100; See appendix page 176.

comma, 100; See appendix page 176.

conjugation, present active indicative, 17; See appendix page 179.

dative case, common use, 24; use demonstrated, 24; accents, 95; See appendix pages 180-183.

declension, see first declension, etc.

diphthongs, 78; See appendix page 175.

direct address, 25, 49, 51; See appendix page 180.

direct object, of sentence, 20; See appendix page 180.

ε, ι, ρ rule, 117; See appendix page 181.

feminine noun, 115, 117, 125, 145, 149, 159; See appendix pages 181-183.

first declension, feminine long alpha, 117; feminine short alpha, 125; feminine eta, 145; plural, 149; circumflex accent in genitive plural, 149; See appendix pages 181-182.

flashcard tips, See appendix page 187.

gamma pronunciation, with γ, κ, or χ, 13.

gender, second declension nouns ending in -os, 101; second declension neuter nouns, 30, 101; articles, 49, 51, 55, 117, 149; first declension long alpha nouns, 117; first declension short alpha nouns, 125; first declension eta nouns, 145; first declension plural nouns, 149; second declension feminine nouns, 159; See appendix pages 180-183.

general accent rules, 85-91; See appendix page 178.

genitive case, common use, 21; use demonstrated, 21; accents, 95, 149; See appendix pages 180-183.

grave accent, 91; See appendix page 177, 178.

he, 17; See appendix page 179.

I, 17; See appendix page 179.

indirect object, of sentence, 24; See appendix page 180.

iota subscript, 78; See appendix page 175.

it, 17; See appendix page 179.

letters, 1-5; See appendix page 175.

masculine noun, 20-25; articles for, 49, 51; See appendix page 183.

mood, of the Greek verb, See appendix page 179.

Greek Workbook - Level 4
Copyright © 1995 by Karen Mohs

185

APPENDIX

Index

moveable v, 23; See appendix page 179.

neuter noun, 30; articles for, 55; See appendix page 183.
ng pronunciation of gamma, 13.
nominative case, common use, 22; use demonstrated, 22, 23; See appendix page 180.
nouns, accent rule, 95; second declension masculine, 20-25; second declension neuter, 30; first declension feminine long alpha, 117; first declension feminine short alpha, 125; first declension eta, 145; first declension plural, 149; second declension feminine, 159; See appendix pages 180-183.
number, expressed by endings of verbs, 17; expressed by endings of nouns, 20-25, 30, 117, 125, 145, 149, 159; See appendix pages 179, 181-183.

o sound of omicron and omega, 7; See appendix page 175.
omega pronunciation, 7; See appendix page 175.
omicron pronunciation, 7; See appendix page 175.

penult, 81; See appendix page 177.
period, 100; See appendix page 176.
possession, 21; See appendix page 180.
present tense, 17; See appendix page 179.
punctuation marks, 100; See appendix page 176.

question mark, 100; See appendix page 176.

rule of noun accent, 95; See appendix page 178.
rule of verb accent, 93; See appendix page 178.

σ, λλ, ζ, ξ, or ψ rule, 125; See appendix page 181.
second declension, masculine, 20-25; neuter, 30; feminine, 159; See appendix page 183.
semicolon, 100; See appendix page 176.

sentence, direct address, 25; direct object, 20; indirect object, 24; possession, 21; subject, 22-23; See appendix page 180.
she, 17; See appendix page 179.
subject, of sentence, 22, 23; See appendix page 180.
syllables, named, 81; length, 82; See appendix page 177.

they, 17; See appendix page 179.

ultima, 81; See appendix page 177, 181, 183.

verbs, accent rule, 93; conjugation, present active indicative, 17; See appendix page 179.
vocative case, common use, 25; use demonstrated, 25; See appendix page 180.
voice, of the Greek verb, See appendix page 179.
vowels, 77; See appendix page 175.

we, 17; See appendix page 179.
word order, 99; See appendix page 176.

you, 17; See appendix page 179.

APPENDIX

Flashcard Tips

1. Remember to practice flashcards daily.

2. Do not move ahead in the workbook if your student is struggling for mastery. Review the flashcards every day until your student is confident and ready to learn more.

3. For each noun and verb ending, there are some "example" words to help your student become familiar with the endings. Please help your student apply these endings to all vocabulary words.

4. When the number of cards becomes too cumbersome to do in one day, remove the cards your student knows without hesitation and put them in an "Occasional Practice" stack. Review the "Occasional Practice" stack once a week.

188

Greek Workbook - Level 4
Copyright © 1995 by Karen Mohs

"Hey, Andrew! Teach Me Some Greek!"
Level 4
Feedback Form

Dear Friend of Greek 'n' Stuff:

Please use the following form to give us your feedback regarding this workbook. Mail your comments to:

> Greek 'n' Stuff
> P.O. Box 882
> Moline, IL 61266-0882

If you prefer, you may send your comments via fax (309-796-2706).

What did you enjoy about this book?

_____

_____

_____

_____

In what ways could this book be more effective?

_____

_____

_____

_____

Circle "yes" beside the Learning Aids which you found helpful in your studies. We would also like to know what you especially liked about each (and/or any suggestions you may have for improvement).

yes   "Answers Only" key _____

yes   "Full Text" key _____

yes   Quizzes/Exams _____

yes   "Flashcards on a Ring" _____

yes   Pronunciation CD/tape _____

yes   Bible Copybook _____

yes   Greek 'n' Stuff's Internet homepage (**www.greeknstuff.com**) with its "Greek and Latin Words of the Month" _____

(front)	(back)
ὁ ἄνθρωπος	(Start on page 7.) (Level 4) **the man** as in <u>The man</u> sees a brother.
ὁ ἀδελφός	(Page 7) (Level 4) **the brother** as in <u>The brother</u> sees a man.
ὁ ἀπόστολος	(Page 7) (Level 4) **the apostle** as in <u>The apostle</u> sees a man.
βλέπω	(Page 7) (Level 4) **I see** as in <u>I see</u> a man.
γινώσκω	(Page 9) (Level 4) **I know** as in <u>I know</u> a man.
καί	(Page 9) (Level 4) **and** as in I see a man <u>and</u> a brother.

(front)	(back)
ὁ δοῦλος	(Page 9) (Level 4) the slave, the servant as in The servant sees a man.
ὁ λόγος	(Page 9) (Level 4) the word as in The word teaches truth.
γράφω	(Page 11) (Level 4) I write as in I write a word.
ὁ υἱός	(Page 11) (Level 4) the son as in The son sees a man.
διδάσκω	(Page 11) (Level 4) I teach as in I teach a word.
ὁ οἶκος	(Page 11) (Level 4) the house as in The house stands on the corner.

(front)	(back)
λέγω	(Page 13) (Level 4) I say as in I say a word.
ὁ νόμος	(Page 13) (Level 4) the law as in The law is written.
ἔχω	(Page 13) (Level 4) I have as in I have a house.
ὁ ἄγγελος	(Page 13) (Level 4) the angel as in The angel sees a house.
λαμβάνω	(Page 15) (Level 4) I take as in I take a gift.
τὸ δῶρον	(Page 15) (Level 4) the gift as in The gift is given.

(front)	(back)
ἀκούω	(Page 15) (Level 4) I hear as in I hear a word.
τὸ ἱερόν	(Page 15) (Level 4) the temple as in The temple has walls.
βλέπεις	(Page 17) (Level 4) you see (singular) as in You see a man.
βλέπει	(Page 17) (Level 4) he sees as in He sees a man.
βλέπομεν	(Page 17) (Level 4) we see as in We see a man.
βλέπετε	(Page 17) (Level 4) you see (plural) as in You see a man.

(front)	(back)
βλέπουσι	(Page 17) (Level 4) **they see** as in <u>They see</u> a man.
λέγεις	(Page 17) (Level 4) **you say** (singular) as in <u>You say</u> a word.
λέγει	(Page 17) (Level 4) **he says** as in <u>He says</u> a word.
λέγομεν	(Page 17) (Level 4) **we say** as in <u>We say</u> a word.
λέγετε	(Page 17) (Level 4) **you say** (plural) as in <u>You say</u> a word.
λέγουσι	(Page 17) (Level 4) **they say** as in <u>They say</u> a word.

(front)	(back)
ἔχεις	(Page 17) (Level 4) you have (singular) as in You have a house.
ἔχει	(Page 17) (Level 4) he has as in He has a house.
ἔχομεν	(Page 17) (Level 4) we have as in We have a house.
ἔχετε	(Page 17) (Level 4) you have (plural) as in You have a house.
ἔχουσι	(Page 17) (Level 4) they have as in They have a house.
τὸν ἄνθρωπον	(Page 20) (Level 4) the man as in I see the man.

(front)	(back)
τοὺς ἀνθρώπους	(Page 20) (Level 4) the men as in I see <u>the men</u>.
τὸν ἀδελφόν	(Page 20) (Level 4) the brother as in I see <u>the brother</u>.
τοὺς ἀδελφούς	(Page 20) (Level 4) the brothers as in I see <u>the brothers</u>.
τὸν υἱόν	(Page 20) (Level 4) the son as in I see <u>the son</u>.
τοὺς υἱούς	(Page 20) (Level 4) the sons as in I see <u>the sons</u>.
τοῦ ἀνθρώπου	(Page 21) (Level 4) of the man as in I see a house <u>of the man</u>.

(front)	(back)
τῶν ἀνθρώπων	(Page 21)　(Level 4) of the men as in I see houses <u>of the men</u>.
τοῦ ἀδελφοῦ	(Page 21)　(Level 4) of the brother as in I see a house <u>of the brother</u>.
τῶν ἀδελφῶν	(Page 21)　(Level 4) of the brothers as in I see houses <u>of the brothers</u>.
τοῦ υἱοῦ	(Page 21)　(Level 4) of the son as in I see a house <u>of the son</u>.
τῶν υἱῶν	(Page 21)　(Level 4) of the sons as in I see houses <u>of the sons</u>.
οἱ ἄνθρωποι	(Page 23)　(Level 4) the men as in <u>The men</u> see a house.

(front)	(back)
οἱ ἀδελφοί	(Page 23) (Level 4) the brothers as in <u>The brothers</u> see a house.
οἱ υἱοί	(Page 23) (Level 4) the sons as in <u>The sons</u> see a house.
τῷ ἀνθρώπῳ	(Page 24) (Level 4) to (or for) the man as in I say a word <u>to the man</u>.
τοῖς ἀνθρώποις	(Page 24) (Level 4) to (or for) the men as in I say a word <u>to the men</u>.
τῷ ἀδελφῷ	(Page 24) (Level 4) to (or for) the brother as in I say a word <u>to the brother</u>.
τοῖς ἀδελφοῖς	(Page 24) (Level 4) to (or for) the brothers as in I say a word <u>to the brothers</u>.

(front)	(back)
τῷ υἱῷ	(Page 24) (Level 4) to (or for) the son as in I say a word <u>to the son</u>.
τοῖς υἱοῖς	(Page 24) (Level 4) to (or for) the sons as in I say a word <u>to the sons</u>.
ἄνθρωπε,	(Page 25) (Level 4) man as in <u>Man</u>, we see a house.
ἄνθρωποι,	(Page 25) (Level 4) men as in <u>Men</u>, we see a house.
ἀδελφέ,	(Page 25) (Level 4) brother as in <u>Brother</u>, we see a house.
ἀδελφοί,	(Page 25) (Level 4) brothers as in <u>Brothers</u>, we see a house.

(front)	(back)
υἱέ,	(Page 25) (Level 4) **son** as in <u>Son</u>, we see a house.
υἱοί,	(Page 25) (Level 4) **sons** as in <u>Sons</u>, we see a house.
τὰ δῶρα	(Page 30) (Level 4) **the gifts** as in <u>The gifts</u> are given. or I give <u>the gifts</u>.
τὰ ἱερά	(Page 30) (Level 4) **the temples** as in <u>The temples</u> have walls. or I see <u>the temples</u>.
ὁ κύριος	(Page 33) (Level 4) **the Lord, the lord** as in <u>The Lord</u> reigns on high.
λύω	(Page 35) (Level 4) **I loose, I destroy** as in <u>I destroy</u> the enemy.

(front)	(back)
ὁ θεός	(Page 37) (Level 4) God, the god as in God loves me.
ἐγείρω	(Page 39) (Level 4) I raise up as in I raise up the man.
ὁ θάνατος	(Page 41) (Level 4) the death as in The death of sin brings victory.
ἄγω	(Page 43) (Level 4) I lead as in I lead the men.
ὁ κόσμος	(Page 45) (Level 4) the world as in The world has many men.
ὁ λίθος	(Page 59) (Level 4) the stone as in The stone is heavy.

(front)	(back)
βάλλω	(Page 61) (Level 4) I throw, I cast, I put as in <u>I throw</u> the ball.
ὁ οὐρανός	(Page 63) (Level 4) the heaven as in <u>The heaven</u> above is vast.
μένω	(Page 65) (Level 4) I remain as in <u>I remain</u> at home.
τὸ τέκνον	(Page 67) (Level 4) the child as in <u>The child</u> is young.
πέμπω	(Page 69) (Level 4) I send as in <u>I send</u> the man.
ὁ τόπος	(Page 71) (Level 4) the place as in <u>The place</u> is cold.

(front)	(back)
φέρω	(Page 73) (Level 4) I bear, I bring as in <u>I bring</u> the gift.
Short Vowels: α ε ο ι υ	(Page 77) (Level 4) **a** in *father* **e** in *get* **o** in *obey* **i** in *pit* **oo** in *good*
Long Vowels: α η ω ι υ	(Page 77) (Level 4) **a** in *father* (held longer) **a** in *late* **o** in *note* **ee** in *feet* **oo** in *good* (held longer)
Diphthongs: αι ει οι αυ	(Page 78) (Level 4) **ai** in *aisle* **a** in *fate* **oi** in *oil* **ow** in *cow*
Diphthongs: ευ ου υι	(Page 78) (Level 4) **eu** in *feud* **oo** in *food* **uee** in *queen*
Breathings: ἐν ἑν	(Page 79) (Level 4) sounds like ***en*** sounds like ***hen***

	(front)	(back)

(front)   **(back)**

Accents:

／　⌢　＼

(Page 80)   (Level 4)

／   acute accent
⌢   circumflex accent
＼   grave accent

Syllables:

ἀ πό στο λος
3   2   1

(Page 81)   (Level 4)

1. ultima
2. penult
3. antepenult

When is a syllable long?

(Page 82)   (Level 4)

1. when it contains a long vowel
2. when it contains any diphthong
   (except αι or οι at the end of a word)

When is a syllable short?

(Page 82)   (Level 4)

1. when it contains a short vowel
2. when it contains αι or οι at the end of the word

Which syllables can have an acute accent?

(Page 85)   (Level 4)

antepenult
penult
ultima

Can the acute accent stand on long or short syllables?

(Page 85)   (Level 4)

both long and short syllables

(front)	(back)
An acute accent cannot stand on the antepenult when the _____ is _____ .	(Page 85) (Level 4) when the ultima is long
An acute accent cannot stand on a long penult when the _____ is _____ .	(Page 85) (Level 4) when the ultima is short
Which syllables can have a circumflex accent?	(Page 87) (Level 4) penult ultima
Can the circumflex accent stand on long or short syllables?	(Page 87) (Level 4) only long syllables
A circumflex accent cannot stand on the penult when the _____ is _____ ?	(Page 87) (Level 4) when the ultima is long
The accent must be a circumflex when the ultima is _____ and the penult is _____ and is accented.	(Page 87) (Level 4) when the ultima is short and the penult is long and is accented

(front)	(back)
Which syllable can have a grave accent?	(Page 91) (Level 4) ultima
When does a word have a grave accent?	(Page 91) (Level 4) when a word has an acute accent on its last syllable and the word is followed immediately by another word
Where does the accent on a verb want to be?	(Page 93) (Level 4) as close to the front of the word as it can be
On a verb: Where is the accent when the ultima is short?	(Page 93) (Level 4) on the antepenult
On a verb: Where is the accent when the ultima is long?	(Page 93) (Level 4) on the penult
Where does the accent on a noun want to be?	(Page 95) (Level 4) It wants to stay where it started. (But sometimes it has to move or change form because of the accent rules.)

(front)	(back)
In Greek, what is this: ,	(Page 100)　　　　　　　　　(Level 4) the comma (like our English comma)
In Greek, what is this: .	(Page 100)　　　　　　　　　(Level 4) the period (like our English period)
In Greek, what is this: ·	(Page 100)　　　　　　　　　(Level 4) the colon (looks like the top half of our English colon) (used like our English colon and semicolon)
In Greek, what is this: ;	(Page 100)　　　　　　　　　(Level 4) the question mark (looks like our English semicolon) (used like our English question mark)
ἡ ἀλήθεια	(Page 101)　　　　　　　　　(Level 4) the truth as in The truth brings peace.
ἡ βασιλεία	(Page 103)　　　　　　　　　(Level 4) the kingdom as in The kingdom is peaceful.

(front)	(back)
ἡ ἡμέρα	(Page 105) (Level 4) **the day** as in The <u>day</u> has come.
ἡ καρδία	(Page 107) (Level 4) **the heart** as in The <u>heart</u> is beating.
ἡ ὥρα	(Page 109) (Level 4) **the hour** as in The <u>hour</u> is late.
ἡ ἐκκλησία	(Page 111) (Level 4) **the church** as in The <u>church</u> has a steeple.
In feminine nouns with ε, ι, or ρ before the final α, the final α is ____.	(Page 117) (Level 4) long
τῆς ἀληθείας	(Page 117) (Level 4) **of the truth** as in The benefits <u>of the truth</u> are many.

(front)	(back)
τῇ ἀληθείᾳ	(Page 117) (Level 4) **to (or for) the truth** as in I give priority <u>to the truth</u>.
τὴν ἀλήθειαν	(Page 117) (Level 4) **the truth** as in I teach <u>the truth</u>.
ἀλήθεια,	(Page 117) (Level 4) **truth** as in <u>Truth</u>, you are of God.
τῆς βασιλείας	(Page 117) (Level 4) **of the kingdom** as in The roads <u>of the kingdom</u> are rocky.
τῇ βασιλείᾳ	(Page 117) (Level 4) **to (or for) the kingdom** as in I write laws <u>for the kingdom</u>.
τὴν βασιλείαν	(Page 117) (Level 4) **the kingdom** as in I see <u>the kingdom</u>.

(front)	(back)
βασιλεία,	(Page 117) (Level 4) kingdom as in <u>Kingdom</u>, you are unconquerable.
τῆς ἡμέρας	(Page 117) (Level 4) of the day as in The ninth hour <u>of the day</u> has passed.
τῇ ἡμέρᾳ	(Page 117) (Level 4) to (or for) the day as in Idolators sing praises <u>to the day</u>.
τὴν ἡμέραν	(Page 117) (Level 4) the day as in I await <u>the day</u>.
ἡμέρα,	(Page 117) (Level 4) day as in <u>Day</u>, I await your coming.
ἡ δόξα	(Page 121) (Level 4) the glory as in <u>The glory</u> of God is everlasting.

(front)	(back)
In feminine nouns with σ, λλ, ζ, ξ, or ψ before the final α, that final α is _____.	(Page 125) (Level 4) short
Τῆς δόξης	(Page 125) (Level 4) of the glory as in Avoid the dangers <u>of the glory</u> of man.
Τῇ δόξῃ	(Page 125) (Level 4) to (or for) the glory as in I sing praises <u>to the glory</u> of God.
Τὴν δόξαν	(Page 125) (Level 4) the glory as in I praise <u>the glory</u> of God.
δόξα,	(Page 125) (Level 4) glory as in <u>Glory</u>, you are man's vanity.
ἡ γραφή	(Page 129) (Level 4) the writing, the Scripture as in <u>The writing</u> is on the wall.

(front)	(back)
ἡ εἰρήνη	(Page 131) (Level 4) **the peace** as in The peace of God reigns in our hearts.
ἡ ἐντολή	(Page 133) (Level 4) **the commandment** as in The commandment was written.
ἡ ζωή	(Page 135) (Level 4) **the life** as in The life of man is short.
ἡ παραβολή	(Page 137) (Level 4) **the parable** as in The parable teaches truth.
ἡ φωνή	(Page 139) (Level 4) **the voice** as in The voice of the mother is gentle.
ἡ ψυχή	(Page 141) (Level 4) **the soul** as in The soul of man is eternal.

(front)	(back)
Besides ending in long α and short α, some feminine nouns end in _____.	(Page 145) (Level 4) η
τῆς γραφῆς	(Page 145) (Level 4) of the writing, of the Scripture as in The message of the Scripture is clear.
τῇ γραφῇ	(Page 145) (Level 4) to (or for) the writing, to (or for) the Scripture as in God gives authority to the Scripture.
τὴν γραφήν	(Page 145) (Level 4) the writing, the Scripture as in I read the Scripture often.
γραφή,	(Page 145) (Level 4) writing, Scripture as in Scripture, you teach me daily.
τῆς φωνῆς	(Page 145) (Level 4) of the voice as in The tone of the voice was pleasant.

(front)	(back)
Τῇ φωνῇ	(Page 145) (Level 4) **to (or for) the voice** as in I give applause <u>to the voice</u>.
Τὴν φωνήν	(Page 145) (Level 4) **the voice** as in I hear <u>the voice</u>.
φωνή,	(Page 145) (Level 4) **voice** as in <u>Voice</u>, sing praises to God.
Τῆς ψυχῆς	(Page 145) (Level 4) **of the soul** as in The future <u>of the soul</u> is eternal.
Τῇ ψυχῇ	(Page 145) (Level 4) **to (or for) the soul** as in Jesus gives life <u>to the soul</u>.
Τὴν ψυχήν	(Page 145) (Level 4) **the soul** as in Jesus saves <u>the soul</u>.

(front)	(back)
ψυχή,	(Page 145) (Level 4) soul as in Soul, hear the voice of God.
αἱ ἀλήθειαι	(Page 149) (Level 4) the truths as in The truths in the Bible are guidelines for life.
τῶν ἀληθειῶν	(Page 149) (Level 4) of the truths as in I rejoice in the goodness of the truths of God.
ταῖς ἀληθείαις	(Page 149) (Level 4) to (or for) the truths as in I give priority to the truths of God.
τὰς ἀληθείας	(Page 149) (Level 4) the truths as in I teach the truths of God.
ἀλήθειαι,	(Page 149) (Level 4) truths as in Truths, you are of God.

(front)	(back)
αἱ δόξαι	(Page 149) (Level 4) the glories as in The glories of man are vain.
τῶν δοξῶν	(Page 149) (Level 4) of the glories as in Avoid the dangers of the glories of men.
ταῖς δόξαις	(Page 149) (Level 4) to (or for) the glories as in I give no reverence to the glories of men.
τὰς δόξας	(Page 149) (Level 4) the glories as in I avoid the glories of men.
δόξαι,	(Page 149) (Level 4) glories as in Glories of man, you are vanity.
αἱ φωναί	(Page 149) (Level 4) the voices as in The voices of the mothers were gentle.

(front)	(back)
τῶν φωνῶν	(Page 149) (Level 4) of the voices as in The tone <u>of the voices</u> was pleasant.
ταῖς φωναῖς	(Page 149) (Level 4) to (or for) the voices as in I give applause <u>to the voices</u>.
τὰς φωνάς	(Page 149) (Level 4) the voices as in I hear <u>the voices</u>.
φωναί,	(Page 149) (Level 4) voices as in <u>Voices</u>, sing praises to God.
ἡ ἔρημος	(Page 153) (Level 4) the desert as in <u>The desert</u> is dry.
ἡ ὁδός	(Page 155) (Level 4) the road, the way as in <u>The road</u> is narrow.

(front)	(back)
Most words ending in *os* are masculine, but some are _____ .	(Page 159) (Level 4) feminine
Τῆς ἐρήμου	(Page 159) (Level 4) of the desert as in The heat <u>of the desert</u> is stifling.
Τῇ ἐρήμῳ	(Page 159) (Level 4) to (or for) the desert as in I wrote a poem <u>to the desert</u>.
Τὴν ἔρημον	(Page 159) (Level 4) the desert as in I see <u>the desert</u>.
ἔρημε,	(Page 159) (Level 4) desert as in <u>Desert</u>, dry our tears.
αἱ ἔρημοι	(Page 159) (Level 4) the deserts as in <u>The deserts</u> of the world are dry.

(front)	(back)
τῶν ἐρημῶν	(Page 159) (Level 4) of the deserts as in The heat <u>of the deserts</u> was stifling.
ταῖς ἐρήμοις	(Page 159) (Level 4) to (or for) the deserts as in I wrote a poem <u>to the deserts</u>.
τὰς ἐρήμους	(Page 159) (Level 4) the deserts as in I crossed <u>the deserts</u>.
ἔρημοι,	(Page 159) (Level 4) deserts as in <u>Deserts</u>, dry our tears.
τῆς ὁδοῦ	(Page 159) (Level 4) of the road, of the way as in The surface <u>of the road</u> is wet.
τῇ ὁδῷ	(Page 159) (Level 4) to (or for) the road, to (or for) the way as in I built a hedge <u>for the road</u>.

(front)	(back)
τὴν ὁδόν	(Page 159) (Level 4) the road, the way as in I paved <u>the road</u>.
ὁδέ,	(Page 159) (Level 4) road, way as in <u>Road</u>, show us the way.
αἱ ὁδοί	(Page 159) (Level 4) the roads, the ways as in <u>The roads</u> are narrow.
τῶν ὁδῶν	(Page 159) (Level 4) of the roads, of the ways as in The surfaces <u>of the roads</u> are wet.
ταῖς ὁδοῖς	(Page 159) (Level 4) to (or for) the roads, to (or for) the ways as in I built hedges <u>for the roads</u>.
τὰς ὁδούς	(Page 159) (Level 4) the roads, the ways as in We paved <u>the roads</u>.

(front)

(back)

ὁδοί,

(Page 159)

(Level 4)

roads, ways

as in
Roads, lead us home.